GUITAR signature licks®

Jim Hall

A Step-By-Step Breakdown
of the Styles and Techniques
of a Jazz Guitar Genius

by Adam Perlmutter

Cover photo by Robin Visotsky

ISBN 978-0-634-08025-8

7777 W. BLUEMOUND RD. P.O. BOX 13819 MILWAUKEE, WI 53213

Copyright © 2009 by HAL LEONARD CORPORATION
International Copyright Secured   All Rights reserved

For all works contained herein:
Unauthorized copying, arranging, adapting, recording, Internet posting, public performance,
or other distribution of the printed or recorded music in this publication is an infringement of copyright.
Infringers are liable under the law.

Visit Hal Leonard Online at
www.halleonard.com

CONTENTS

Page	Title	CD Track
4	Introduction	
4	Discography	
5	The Recording	
5	Equipment	
	Tuning	1
6	**(All of a Sudden) My Heart Sings**	2–3
12	**Angel Eyes**	4–5
19	**Autumn Leaves**	6–7
26	**Big Blues**	8–10
34	**My Man's Gone Now**	11–12
39	**Prelude to a Kiss**	13–16
44	**Scrapple from the Apple**	17–19
50	**St. Thomas**	20–21
56	**Tangerine**	22–23
61	**Things Ain't What They Used to Be**	24–25
65	**Without a Song**	26–28
71	**You'd Be So Nice to Come Home To**	29–32
78	Guitar Notation Legend	

INTRODUCTION

Jim Hall (1930–) was steeped in classical music before he came to jazz. Hall attended the Cleveland Institute of Music, then moved to Los Angeles, California, where he studied nylon-string guitar with Vincente Gómez. While on the West Coast, he began to make a name for himself as a jazz guitarist, playing in the quintet of drummer Chico Hamilton, from 1955 to 1956, and in the trio of reed player Jimmy Giuffre, from 1956–1959. He also worked with modern improvisers such as pianist John Lewis and alto saxophonist Lee Konitz, and in 1960 toured South America (where he was exposed to bossa nova) with singer Ella Fitzgerald.

Around the same time, Hall moved to New York City, where through several intense collaborations, he was established as one of the world's most sophisticated jazz guitarists. From 1961 to 1962, he was a member of the tenor saxophonist Sonny Rollins's great quartet, with which he recorded the seminal album *The Bridge*. In the '60s Hall co-led a quartet with trumpeter Art Farmer; he also recorded with the quartet of alto saxophonist Paul Desmond and found ideal duet partners in pianist Bill Evans and bassist Ron Carter. With Evans, Hall recorded two albums, *Undercurrent* (1962) and *Intermodulation* (1966), two of the most intimate and beautiful recordings in all of jazz. (From *Intermodulation*, see the transcription of "My Man's Gone Now," on page 34.)

It was while performing in these fertile contexts that Hall found his own voice, an understated modern style characterized by melodic finesse, harmonic sophistication, and structural awareness—a logical extension of the language developed by such jazz-guitar pioneers as Charlie Christian, Wes Montgomery, and Django Reinhardt. This approach has been of profound influence to countless modern guitarists, including Hall's student Bill Frisell, who sounds radically different than Hall, but has a strikingly similar guitar conception. Hall's approach is best witnessed on the excellent albums he has recorded under his own name, including *Concierto* (1975), *Jim Hall Live!* (1976), and *All Across the City* (1989), transcriptions from all of which can be found on the following pages.

Besides being one of jazz's premier guitarists, Hall is a celebrated arranger and composer. In 1997, he won the New York Jazz Critics Circle Award for Best Jazz Composer/Arranger; his composition for jazz quartet and string quartet, "Quartet Plus Four," earned the Jazzpar Prize in Denmark, and his works for string, brass, and vocal ensembles can be heard on the albums *Textures* (1997) and *By Arrangement* (1998). In 2004, the Baltimore Symphony Orchestra debuted Hall's *Peace Movement*, a concerto for guitar and orchestra, dedicated to the cause of international harmony. That same year, for all his accomplishments as a composer, arranger, and performer, Hall was named a Jazz Master by the National Endowment for the Arts.

One of Hall's most recent projects, *Hemispheres*, was recorded with Bill Frisell and features one disc of duets and a second disc that adds the rhythm section of bassist Scott Colley and drummer Joey Baron. The album is available at Hall's Web site (www.jimhallmusic.com), where a fan can catch of glimpse of what goes into the creation of the guitarist's recent projects. Meanwhile, when not composing or working with his own trio, Hall—ever the adventurous artist—has been playing with various modern improvisers, including saxophonists Joe Lovano and Greg Osby, and guitarist Pat Metheny. For now in the sixth decade of his career, Hall remains as vital a musician as ever.

DISCOGRAPHY

The selections on the accompanying CD are based on the following recordings:

ALL ACROSS THE CITY—Concord Jazz: "Big Blues"
ALONE TOGETHER—Milestone: "Autumn Leaves," "St. Thomas"
BALLAD ESSENTIALS—Concord Jazz: "Prelude to a Kiss"
CONCIERTO—CTI: "You'd Be So Nice to Come Home To"

HALLMARKS: THE BEST OF JIM HALL—Concord Jazz: "(All of a Sudden) My Heart Sings"
INTERMODULATION—Verve: "My Man's Gone Now"
JAZZ GUITAR: JIM HALL TRIO—Pacific: "Tangerine," "Things Ain't What They Used to Be"
JIM HALL LIVE!—A&M: "Angel Eyes," "Scrapple from the Apple"
THE BRIDGE—RCA: "Without a Song"

THE RECORDING

Doug Boduch: guitar
Warren Wiegratz: piano and keyboards
Tom McGirr: bass
Scott Schroedl: drums

Recorded at Beathouse Music, Milwaukee, WI
Produced by Jim Reith

EQUIPMENT

Although Jim Hall has never been much of a gearhead, he has always played nice instruments. The earliest guitar with which Hall was associated was the black Gibson Les Paul Custom he played with Chico Hamilton. Reportedly, in 1956 he traded that axe for Howard Roberts' sunburst Gibson ES-175, which he still owns today but rarely uses. (You can see this very box on the cover of *Jazz Guitar: Jim Hall Trio*.) The ES-175's 24.75"-scale-length rosewood fretboard allowed Hall to play chords that required a large fret-hand stretch. Its comfortable, 16" laminated maple body held up well on the road while—in conjunction with a single P-90 (single-coil) pickup—providing Hall with a consistently warm tone.

Hall's next main guitar was made for him by master luthier Jimmy D'Aquisto. Hall is seen playing this exquisite box, with its lovely reddish orange top, on the cover of *All Across the City*. The guitar is based on the ES-175—it has similar dimensions, as well as a single DeArmond/Guild humbucker pickup—but is entirely handmade and contains D'Aquisto's trademark ornamentation, such as the "New Yorker" headstock.

New York luthier/repairman Roger Sadowsky had maintained Hall's D'Aquisto for approximately 15 years before the two decided to collaborate on a guitar that would be affordable for the working jazz guitarist. Introduced in 2003, Sadowsky's Jim Hall Signature Model is inspired by the D'Aquisto, with a laminated 16" body; 24.75"-scale-length ebony fretboard; modernist ornamentation; and ebony tuning buttons, pickguard, knobs, bridge, and tailpiece. Like Hall's style, the Sadowsky guitar is at once spare and elegant.

Hall has a light touch and therefore favors light-gauge flatwound strings (.011–.050). Because he likes to string-bend, to sound like a horn, Hall sometimes uses an unwound .019 third string, as opposed to the standard .022. He's also known to carry a pocketful of assorted picks—thick ones for fat single-note lines and thin ones for brisk strumming, etc.

As for amplification, early in his career, Hall favored a Gibson GA-50 with its valve-tube power, two speakers (12" and 8"), and old-radio appearance. This unit didn't hold up to the rigors of touring, though, so Hall has since managed to duplicate the sound with several different amplifiers, including a solid-state Polytone Mini-Brute, a Walter Woods model, and a Harry Kolbe GP-1 preamp and speaker cabinet.

(ALL OF A SUDDEN) MY HEART SINGS

(Hallmarks: The Best of Jim Hall, 2006)

English Words and Music by Harold Rome, Jamblan and Laurent Herpin
French Words by Jamblan

Figure 1—Head

In the small groups of reed player Jimmy Giuffre and drummer Chico Hamilton, Hall established himself as an ensemble player of uncommon sensitivity. But some of Hall's best work has been with one of his own trios, consisting of bassist Rufus Reid and drummer Terry Clarke. Originally released on 1981's *Circles*, "(All of a Sudden) My Heart Sings" is a nice Latin take on a great standard, on which the trio is augmented by pianist Don Thompson.

In his 32-bar intro, Hall—supported solely by Clarke—plays an ultra-modern chord-melody solo. Bars 1–12 find Hall playing a series of chords that is related to the original melody (as you'll see in bar 33) via contour—the top voice of each subsequent chord pair moves up a 2nd. For example, the note D is common to both F#m7+5 and Ab7#11, and, a major 2nd higher, E is common to G6 and Bb7#11. Also, note that each m7+5 chord can be alternatively viewed as an add9 chord with the 3rd in the bass. So, F#m7+5 could be thought of as Dadd9/F#, which, incidentally, is related to the Ab7#11 by a tritone.

Beginning in bar 13, Hall's harmonic adventurousness continues as he travels through a bunch of distant keys: The Abm11 and Db7b13#9 chords belong to Gb major, followed by a sudden modulation to D major from bar 14's D6/9 chord through bar 15's F#m7 chord. On beat 3 of bar 16, the F#7b13 acts as the V chord, setting up a short visit to the key of B minor. Then, starting at the end of bar 18, Hall moves to the key of F# minor, starting with the III chord, Amaj7. In bar 21, notice how Hall holds the highest note, B, while he plays a series of chromatically descending chords underneath; this move is transposed down a whole step in bar 23.

Moving his way toward the head, Hall slips through a few more keys: Eb major (Fm9–Bb13b5–Ebmaj7–Eb7), B major (F#13–F#7b13–B9–B7#11), and D major (Em7–A9–D9sus4). Beginning at the end of bar 31, Hall smoothly moves the D9sus4 chord chromatically down to C13sus4, where it acts as the V chord, setting up the F major tune.

The head, which begins in bar 33, has a 32-bar AB song form, in which each section is 16 bars long. In contrast to Hall's harmonically complex intro, the changes here are diatonically straightforward—lots of I–VI–ii–V (Fmaj7–Dm7–Gm7–C7) progressions. Throughout, Hall decorates the original melody with melodic and rhythmic flourishes, such as the rapid scalar line on beat 4 of bar 40, the chromatic lower-neighbor tone (fourth-fret B) of bar 46, and the extensive syncopation of bar 49.

A Hall hallmark is found in bar 47: he plays a note (in this case, the sixth-fret F) and follows it with the same note on a lower, adjacent string, often sliding into the note from the distance of a major 2nd (here, from the eighth-fret Eb to the tenth-fret F). Hall does the same with the A notes in bar 59, the G notes in bar 61, and the F notes in bar 63.

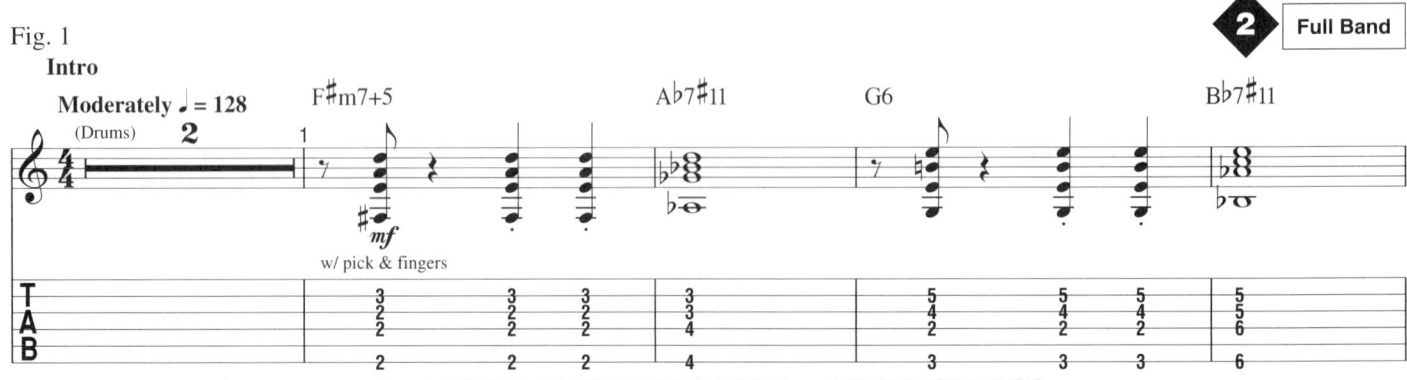

Copyright © 1941, 1944 FRANCE MUSIC CORP. and HAROLD ROME MUSIC
Copyright Renewed
All Rights for FRANCE MUSIC CORP. in English Speaking Countries Controlled and Administered by UNIVERSAL MUSIC CORP.
All Rights for HAROLD ROME MUSIC Controlled and Administered by HELENE BLUE MUSIQUE LTD.
All Rights Reserved   Used by Permission

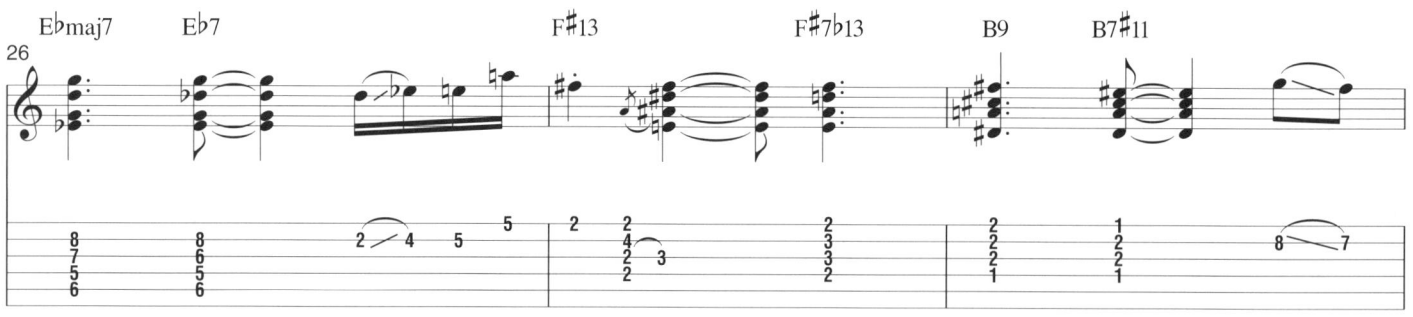
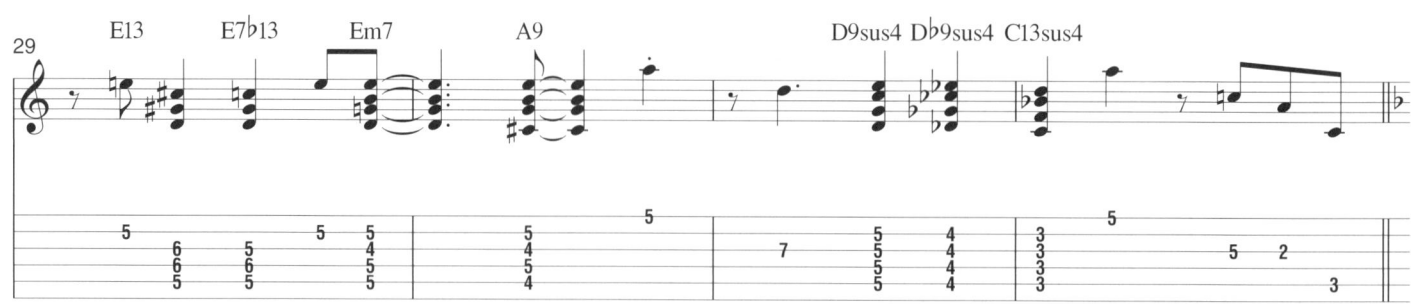
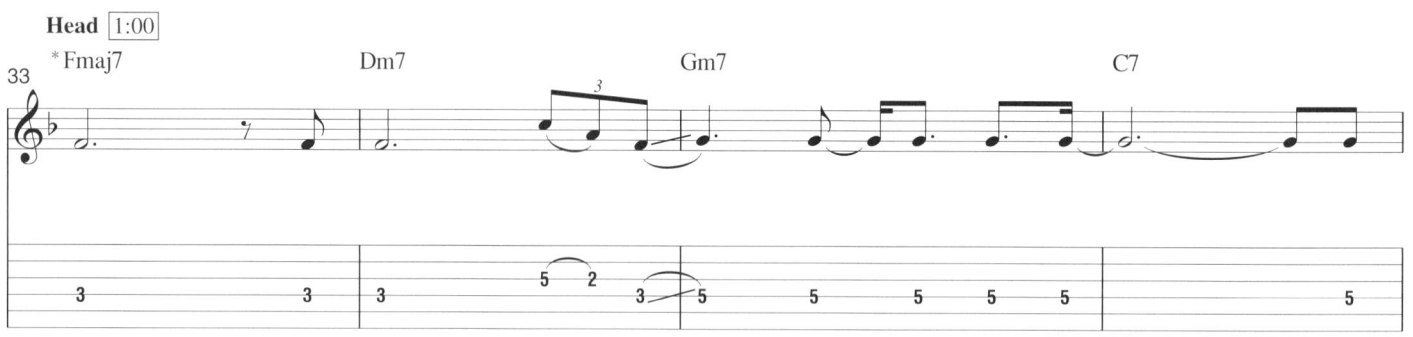

*Chord symbols reflect basic harmony.

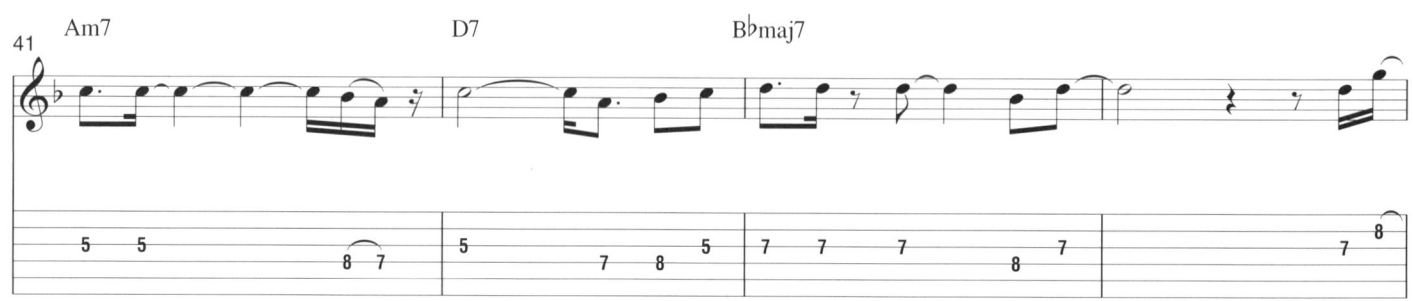

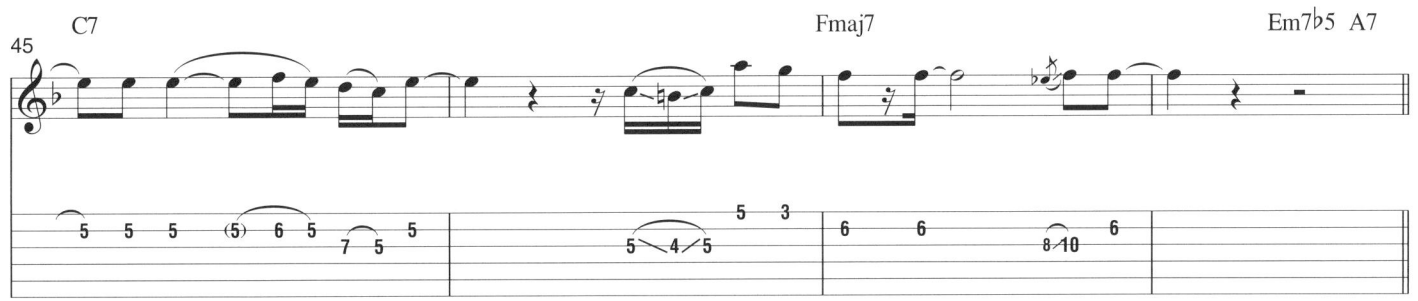
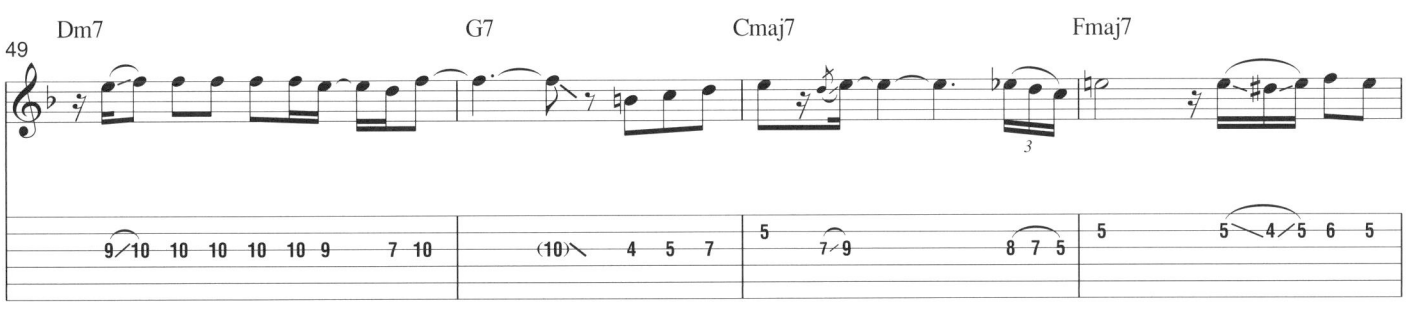
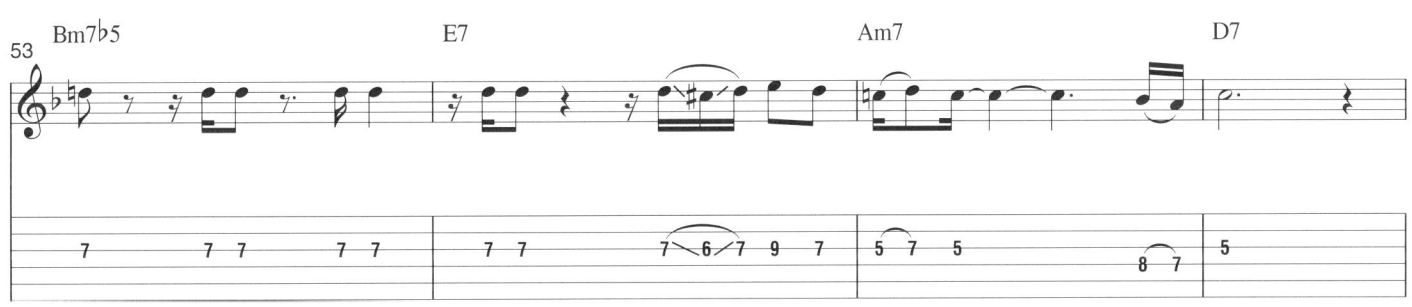
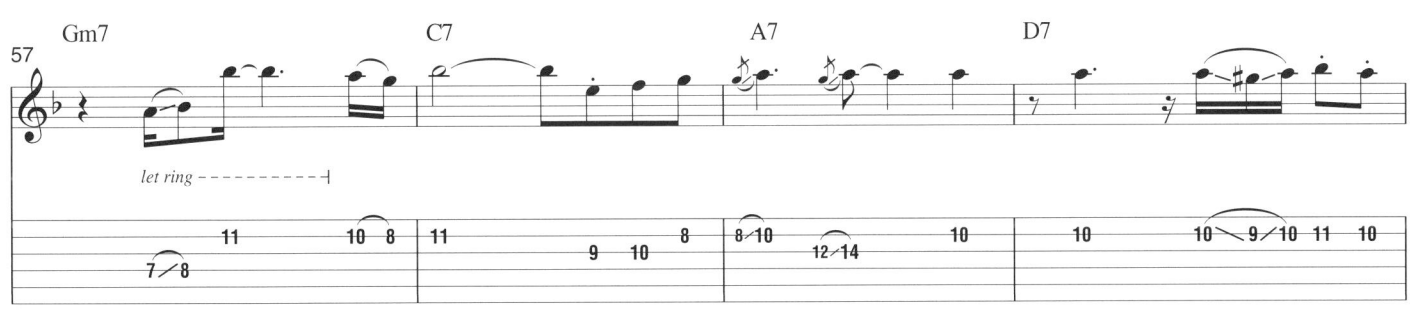
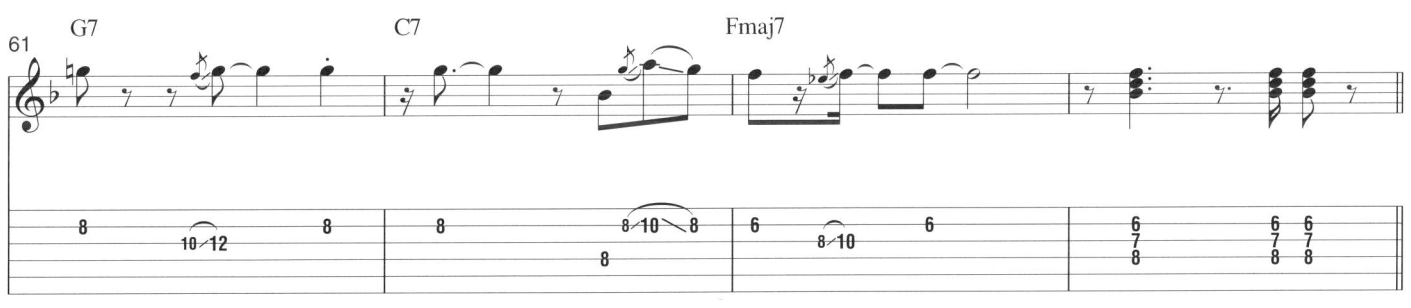

Figure 2—Solo

As he did in his chord-melody intro, Hall starts out his solo with a series of phrases that mirror the ascending contour of the original melody. While he plays each phrase—based entirely on the F major scale (F–G–A–Bb–C–D–E)—using mostly stepwise movement, he still manages to sound supremely melodic. Beginning in bar 13, Hall changes things up with a series of descending 3rds, both major and minor, within the scale. Then, he kicks off bar 15 with another F-to-F move, followed in bar 16 by a tastefully bluesy line, with a half-step pre-bend—unusual for a jazz guitarist—on beat 3.

In the next section, from bars 18–24, Hall has a conversation with himself. He plays a short, diatonic idea (save for the occasional chromatic approach tone) on string 1, answering it with a similar idea on strings 3 and 2. This leads into a descending F major line with a b5 (Cb) passing tone, which then works its way back up to the tenth-fret A; Hall—unafraid to work a single note—explores the A in syncopated fashion in bars 27–28.

Beginning in bar 30, Hall closes his solo in the opposite direction from which it began, with a beautiful, descending series of diatonic 6ths. Then, at the end of bar 32, he plays an ascending scalar line, ending on the chromatic note G#, to set up his restatement of the head.

Fig. 2

Solo 3:45

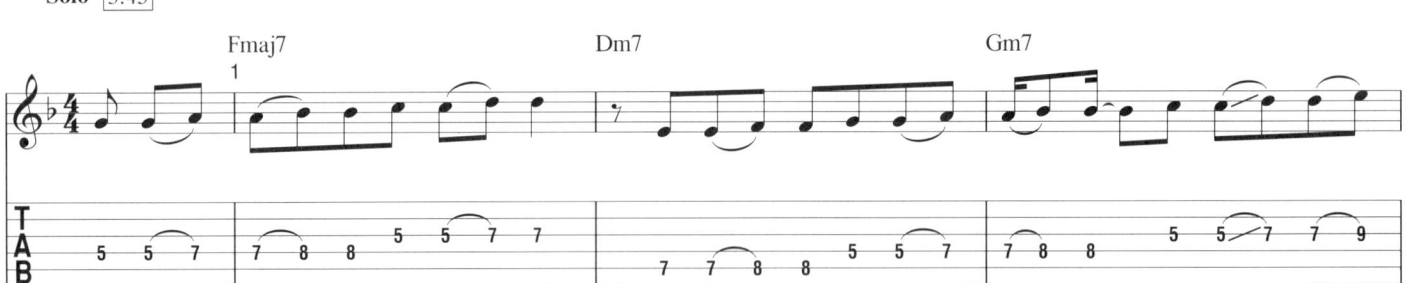

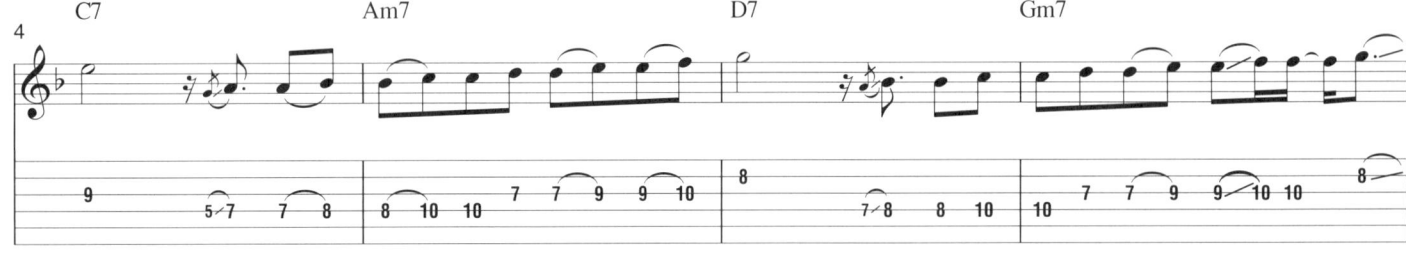

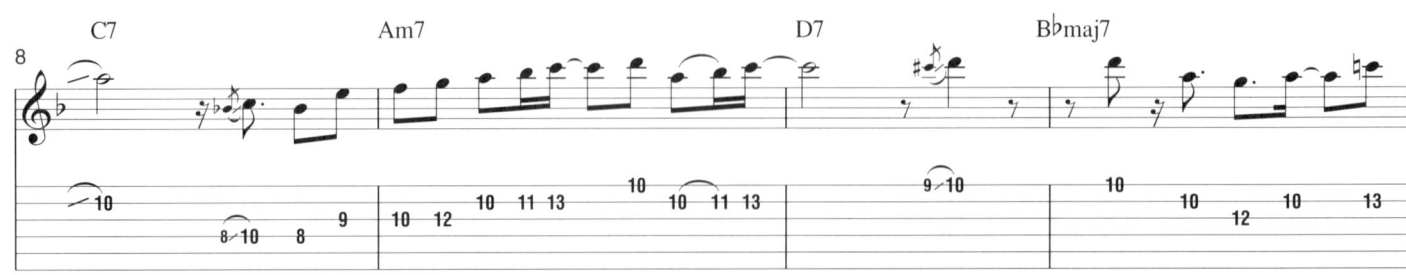

ANGEL EYES
(*Jim Hall Live!*, 1976)
Words by Earl Brent
Music by Matt Dennis

Figure 3—Intro, Head, and Solo (Chorus 1)

While many of Jim Hall's studio recordings show the guitarist to be thoughtful and well-mannered, in concert he has been known to play with abandon. This side of Hall can be heard on *Jim Hall Live!*, one of his finest live recordings, taken from a series of dates in 1975 at Toronto's Bourbon Street. The recording finds Hall in top form, paired with bassist Don Thompson and drummer Terry Clarke.

One of the highlights of the album is a Latin-tinged take of the jazz standard "Angel Eyes," which was originally a 32-bar AABA song. Hall & Co. double the tune's harmonic rhythm, so that the form is now 64 bars in length. (A chord that originally occupied two beats now gets four beats, an entire bar.) Hall starts things off by moving a barred Am7 shape in parallel fashion against the open A string, resulting in some interesting polychordal harmony, such as the D♭/A chord (voiced A–A♭–D♭–F, low to high) on beat 1 of bar 2 and the B/A (A–F♯–B–D♯) on beat 1 of bar 4. He also throws various dominant and diminished chord voicings into the mix, including the partial E7♯9 (A♭/G♯–D–G) in the last part of bar 2 and D♭° (A♭–D–F) on beat 1 of bar 6.

After closing out the intro with the same Am7 chord with which he started, Hall takes the head (beginning at bar 17). He sticks pretty close to the original melody, adding his own idiosyncratic touches here and there. One such Hall-ism involves placing an octave-based idea at the end of a phrase—a striking, broken-octave fill appears in bars 23–24; a variation of this, in bar 39; and, in bar 72, a semi-chromatic descending line played in fully voiced octaves. Throughout, there's a strong blues feel, especially in bar 32's fill, which comes from the A minor pentatonic scale (A–C–D–E–G), albeit unpredictably ordered. A subtler touch involves ending certain phrases with a 12th-fret harmonic on string 5 (see bars 30, 46, and 78), which lends a nice timbral contrast to the fretted notes.

Beginning in bar 49, Hall uses a neat trick that effectively separates the bridge from the A-section: while holding selected melody notes (upstemmed), he adds chord stabs (downstemmed), not unlike a pianist would do with two hands. Also, Hall ventures a little farther from the melody in this section—in bar 53, check out the improvised, angular line that begins with a major 7th (B♭ to A) leap. These unique details give the listener a taste of what's to come in Hall's excellent solo.

In the first A-section of his first chorus, Hall introduces an A minor pentatonic idea, and then sees it through various permutations. He keeps it simple here; the only noticeable jazzy melodic content is the Am11 arpeggio (A–C–E–G–B–D) in bars 108–109. Throughout, Hall interjects some of the same chord voicings as found in the intro, most often the E7♯9 chord. At the same time, he uses space wisely; for example, see the rests in bars 107–108 and 116–117.

Hall steps out melodically in the bridge of the first chorus. In bars 122–123, he plays a 6th-based motif that reappears later in the solo, and in bars 125–127, he smoothly hits a variety of interesting note choices: the 7 (F♯) on the Gm7 chord (the absence of a pianist gives Hall harmonic leeway), the ♯9 (E♭/D♯) on C7, and the ♯11 (B) on Fmaj7. Beginning in bar 128, Hall plays a fleetingly-fingered line involving chromatic lower-neighbor tones. This leads directly into a witty reference to Duke Ellington's "Raincheck" in bars 129–131. Quotation is an indispensable improvisational tool, and Hall masterfully adjusts the melodic contour of "Raincheck" to suit the changes at hand, sailing with ease into the ♭7 (A) of the B7 chord and the 3rd (G♯) of the Emaj7 chord.

Copyright © 1946 (Renewed) by Music Sales Corporation (ASCAP)
International Copyright Secured   All Rights Reserved
Reprinted by Permission

In bar 136, Hall eases into some additional pentatonic material, again yielding to some jazzier content—a C13 arpeggio (voiced B♭–E–A–C–E) in bar 142, followed by some pungent altered chords in bar 144. In bar 145, note that Hall plays a rootless D9 chord (voiced F♯–C–E–A), which in this context functions as an Am6 chord (A–C–E–F♯, in root position.) Hall ends his first chorus, in bar 151, with an idea he explores more fully in "St. Thomas": he pits fretted notes on string 4—in this case, from the A Dorian mode (A–B–C–D–E–F♯–G)—against the open G string.

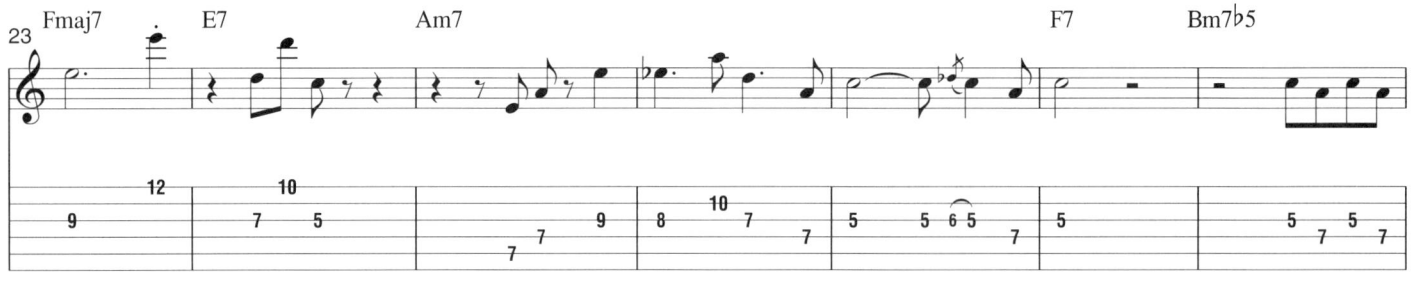

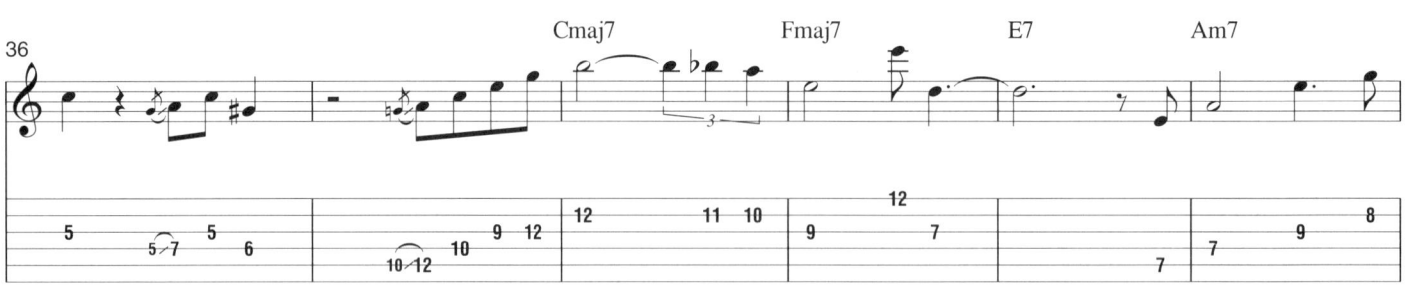
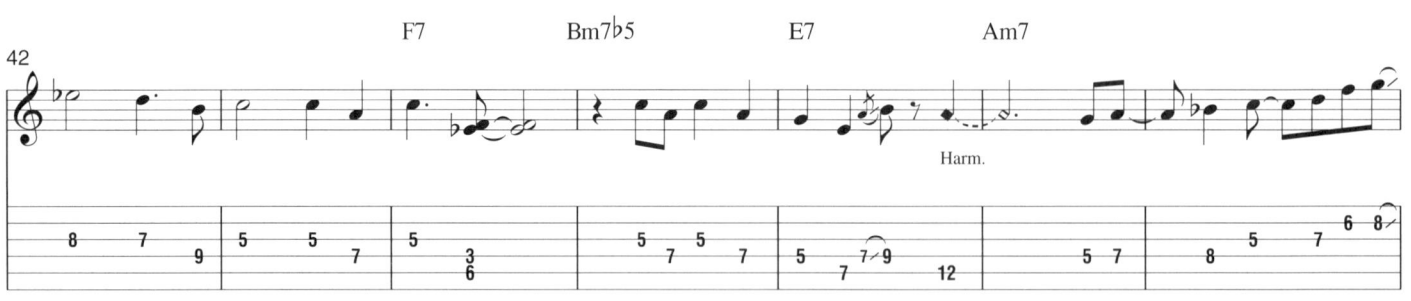

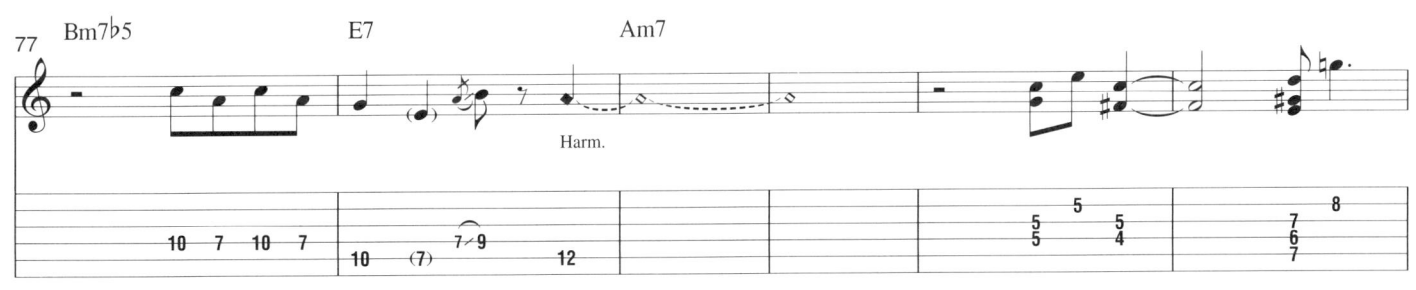

Solo 1st Chorus 2:02

16

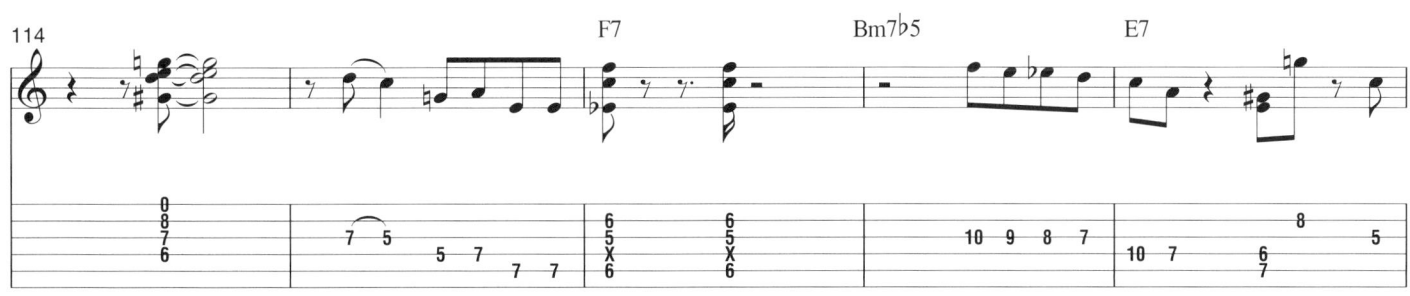
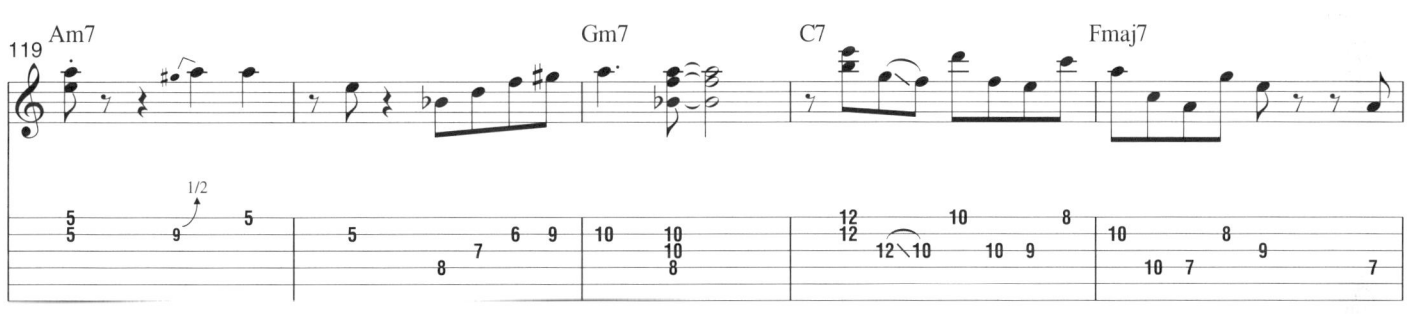

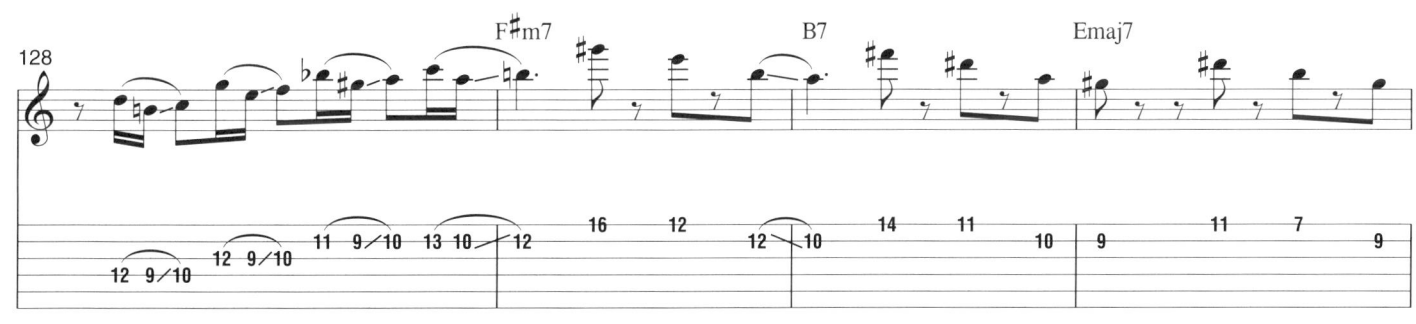

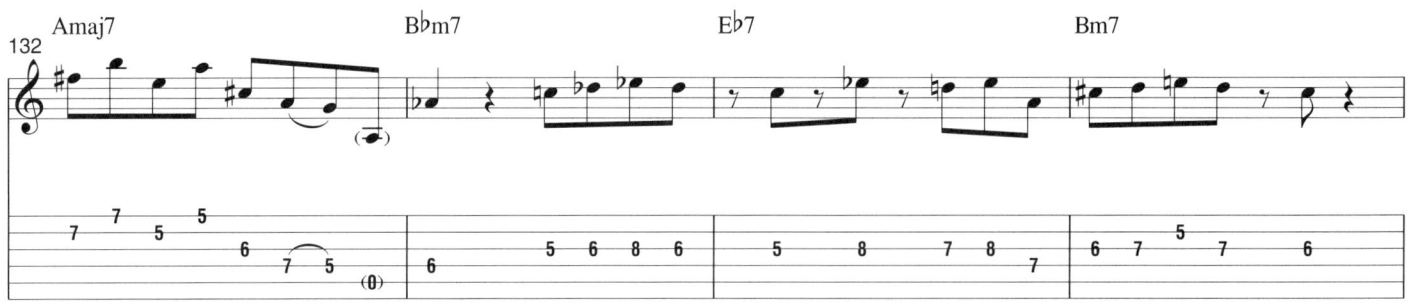
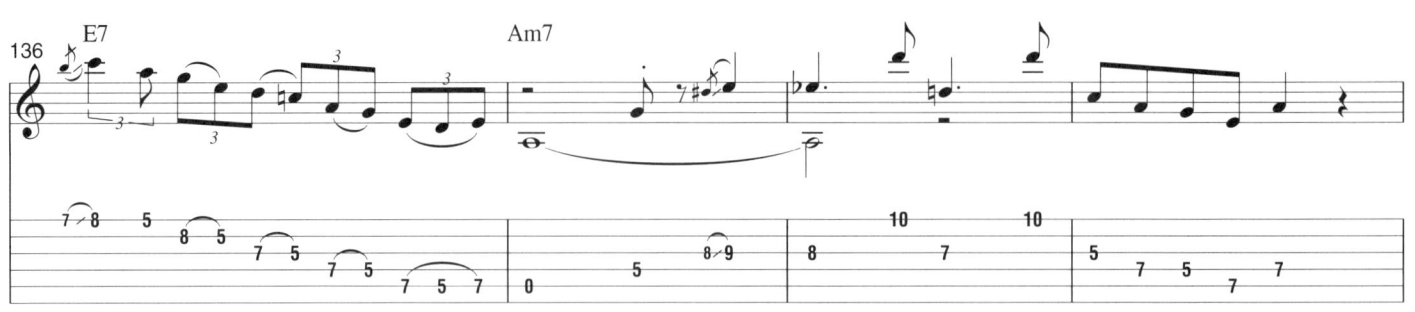
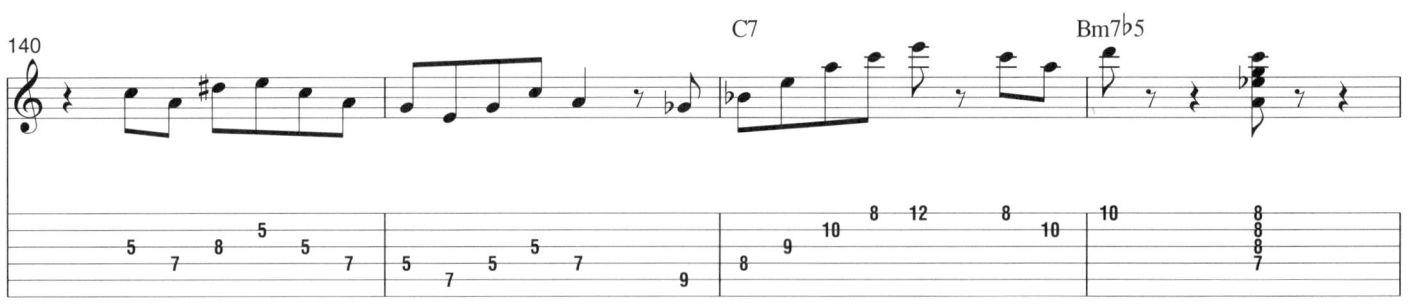
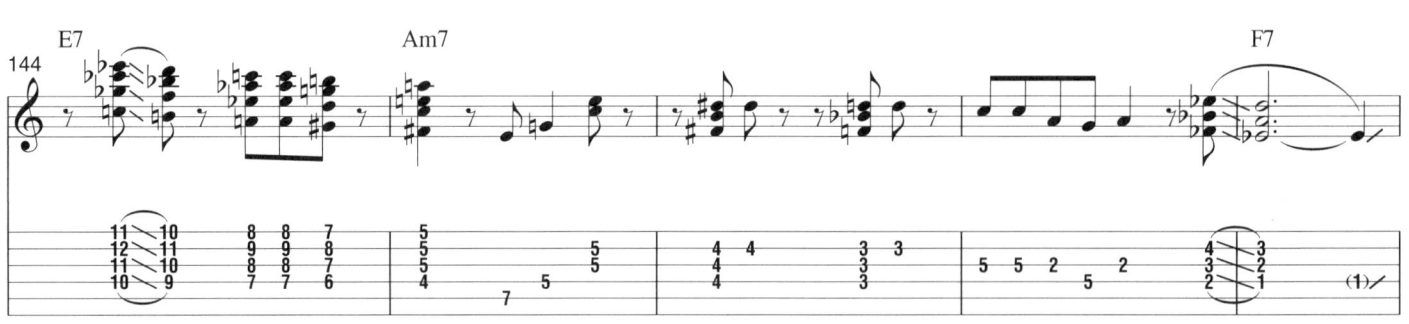
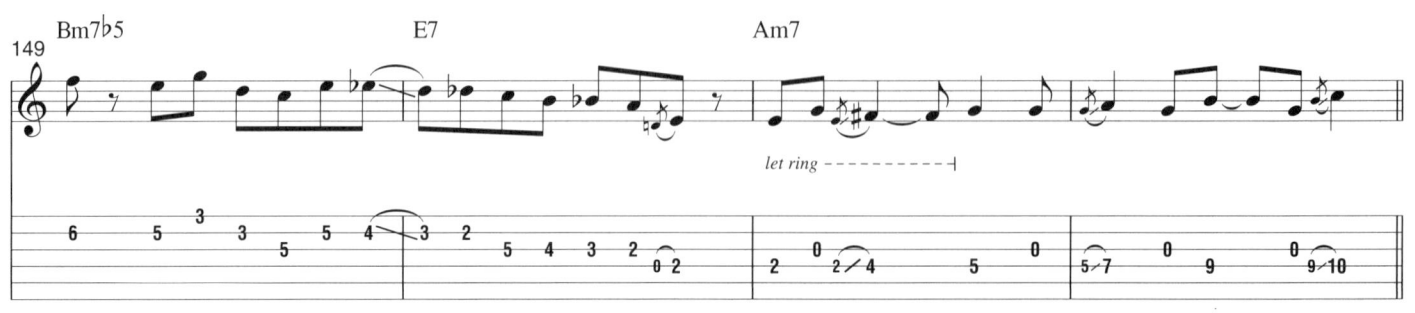

AUTUMN LEAVES
(*Alone Together*, 1972)

English lyric by Johnny Mercer
French lyric by Jacques Prevert
Music by Joseph Kosma

Figure 4—Head and Solo

In addition to two intimate records with pianist Bill Evans, Jim Hall's catalog boasts several excellent duet recordings with bassist Ron Carter: *Alone Together* (1972), *Live at Village West* (1982), and *Telephone* (1984). Each album showcases the uncanny musical telepathy shared by Hall and Carter; particularly noteworthy is the duo's deft rhythmic interplay.

From *Alone Together*, "Autumn Leaves" is based on a 32-bar song form, played here in the key of G minor. As usual, Hall adds his own special touches to the head. In the first several bars, he places some new notes underneath the original melody; for example, in bar 2, he props up the G and A notes with a pair of Fs. Some other touches: Hall approaches bar 9's E♭ note with an A♭° triad (A♭–C♭/B–E♭♭/D), articulated with a downward rake. In bar 14, he adds a tasty fill from the G blues scale (G–B♭–C–D♭–D–F). Hall beefs up the melody in bars 16–21 with some octaves on strings 2 and 4. Note the hip harmonic move in bars 22–23: a single chord shape—containing stacked 4ths with a major 3rd on top—is used to negotiate a V–I (F7–B♭maj7) change. Over the F7 chord, this shape, which is moved down a major 2nd, contains some choice dissonances: the ♭13 (D♭), ♯9 (G♯/A♭), and ♭9 (G♭). Moved down an additional half step, the shape sounds consonant, forming a B♭maj9 chord (voiced C–F–B♭–D).

At the end of bar 24, Hall adds some more arpeggio work to the original melody, approaching bar 25's E♭ with a broken E♭maj7 chord (E♭–G–B♭–D). Also note the sneaky, chromatic quintuplet on beat 4 of bar 25, a characteristic inflection of Hall's. In bars 26–29, Hall changes things up with a keyboard-like texture: underneath a melody on string 1, he plays chords on strings 3–4. Each two-note voicing contains only the essential harmonic information—the chord's 3rd and 7th—which facilitates some smooth voice leading. In bar 27, for instance, the Gm7 chord's ♭3rd (eighth-fret B♭) becomes the C7 chord's ♭7th, and the Gm7's ♭7th (tenth-fret F) is moved down a half step, becoming the C7 chord's 3rd (ninth-fret E). Beginning in the last half of bar 31, Hall closes out the head with a line from the G half-whole diminished scale (G–A♭–B♭–B–C♯–D–E–F), which implies an altered G7 chord, containing the ♭9 (A♭), ♯9 (A♯/B♭), and ♭5/♯11 (D♭/C♯).

In his first solo chorus, in bar 34, Hall establishes a one-bar rhythmic motif: an eighth note rest, followed by a dotted quarter note and a half note. He carries the motif through the first half of bar 39, sticking to notes that clearly define each chord. For example, in bar 35, Hall highlights the 3rd (D) and 7th (A) of the B♭maj7 chord (B♭–D–F–A). In bar 39, Carter sets up a tritone substitution—he plays a D♭ (implying a D♭7 chord) in place of the expected G (Gm7). Hall responds smartly, with notes from a D♭9♯11 chord (D♭–F–A♭–C♭–E♭–G). Then, in bars 41–44, he revisits the rhythmic motif, neatly approaching the second note of each bar by a half step.

In bar 47, Hall plays a line drawn from the G harmonic minor scale (G–A–B♭–C–D–E♭–F♯), which implies a Gm(maj7) chord (G–B♭–D–F♯). He then plays a blues fill similar to the one found in the head, setting it up with a neat trick: he simultaneously plays a D note on string 2 and a C♯ note on string 3, then slides the C♯ up a fret, to match the pitch of the higher note. In bars 50, 52, and 54, Hall plays another rhythmic motif—two eighth notes followed by an eighth note rest, then another eighth note—on string 5, answered by some chromatic blueness in bars 51, 53, and the end of 54. Then, he transposes the rhythmic motif to a higher register in bars 55 and 56, focusing on the 7th (A) of the B♭maj7 chord and the root (E♭ of E♭maj7).

In bars 57–60, Hall returns to the octave texture of the head, playing syncopated pairs from the G harmonic minor scale with a few chromatic passing tones thrown in—C♭ in bar 57 and A♭ in bar 59. He wraps up his chorus the same way he ended the head, with a G-diminished-scale line, this time played in a higher octave.

Hall gets a bit more melodically adventurous in his second chorus. In bar 66, for example, he hits both the ♯9 (A♭/G♯) and ♭9 (G♭) of the F7 chord; in the second half of bar 67, he makes a major 7th leap from A♭ to G, implying a B♭13 chord (B♭–D–F–A♭–C–E♭–G), then hits the ♭13 (G♭) on beat 4, followed by a trademark upwards rake. Chromatic passing tones abound in bars 68–69, then, in bar 70, as he did with the F7 chord, Hall incorporates both the ♯9 (F/E♯) and ♭9 (E♭) of D7.

In bars 71–72, Hall works with another rhythmic motif—a quarter note followed by a pair of eighth-note triplets (tied in the center), all within the G melodic-minor scale (G–A–B♭–C–D–E–F♯). On beat 3 of bar 72 he lands on a B♮, implying a G7 chord, then follows it up with the notes of a B°7 arpeggio (B–D–F–A♭), functioning as a G7♭9 in this context, and resolving smoothly down a half step to the 5th (G) of Cm7 in bar 73.

Beginning at the end of bar 73 and extending till bar 76, Hall works with some more triplet-based motifs, each one with an ascending stepwise series of mostly diatonic notes. Then, in bar 80, he plays some more octave-based lines, surrounding them with some four-note block chords. Check out Hall's excellent voice leading—in bars 81–82, the top two notes of the A7♭13 and D7♯9 chords remain constant (A is the root of A7♭13 and the 5th of D7♯9, F (E♯) is the ♭13 of A7♭13 and the ♯9 of D7♯9), while the bottom two notes move down a half step each. Some final highlights of the second chorus: in bar 86, another major 7th leap, from G♭ to F, occurs, implying an F7♭9 chord (F–A–C–E♭–G♭). In bars 92–93, Hall revisits the piano-like texture he explored in the head, harmonizing the original melody notes B♭ and A with some bold, parallel 7♯9 chords. In bars 95–96, Hall closes out the chorus with notes belonging to a G7♭13 chord (G–B–D–F–E♭), which is similar to the implied D♭9♯11 chord (D♭–F–A♭–C♭–E♭–G) of bars 39 and 40.

Beginning in bar 97, Hall's final chorus incorporates all of the elements involved in the previous two choruses, including hip altered lines (bar 102), smartly voiced blocked chords (bars 104–105), and assorted chromatics (bar 118). To negotiate the ii–V–I (Am7♭5–D7–Gm7) progression in bars 113–115, Hall does something very cool: he plays whole tone–based dyads, moving everything down a half step for each subsequent chord. He ends the solo simply, with some shell (3rd-and-7th) voicings in bar 127.

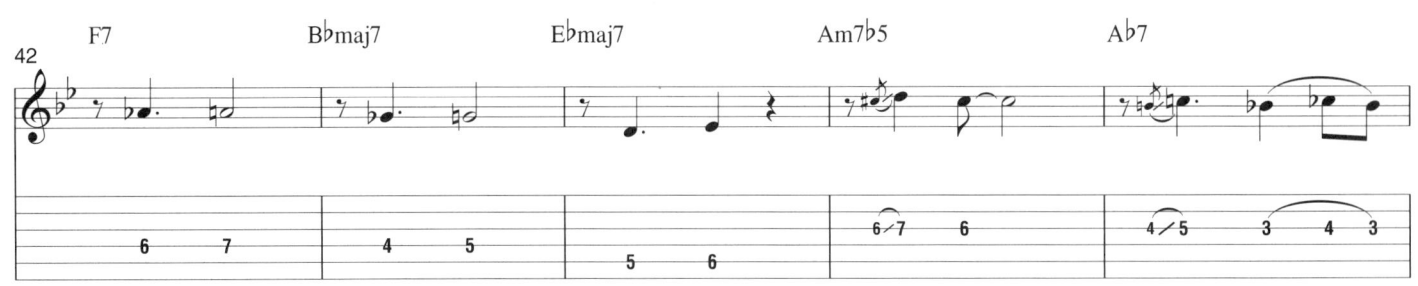
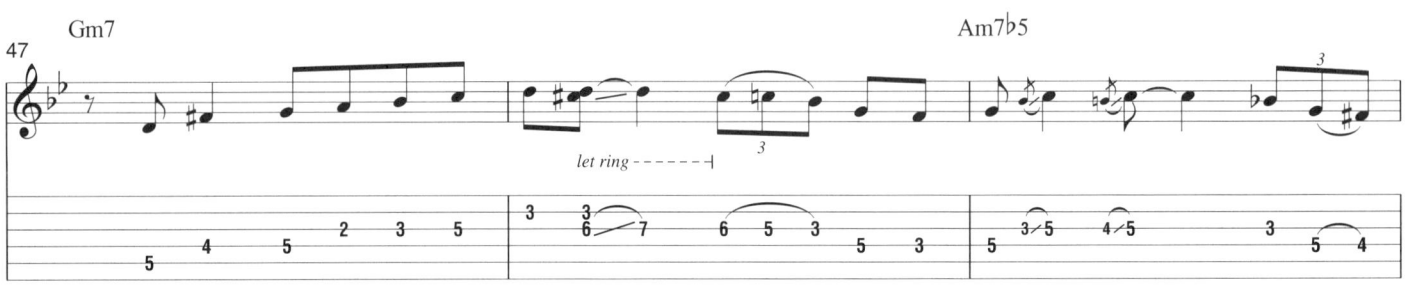
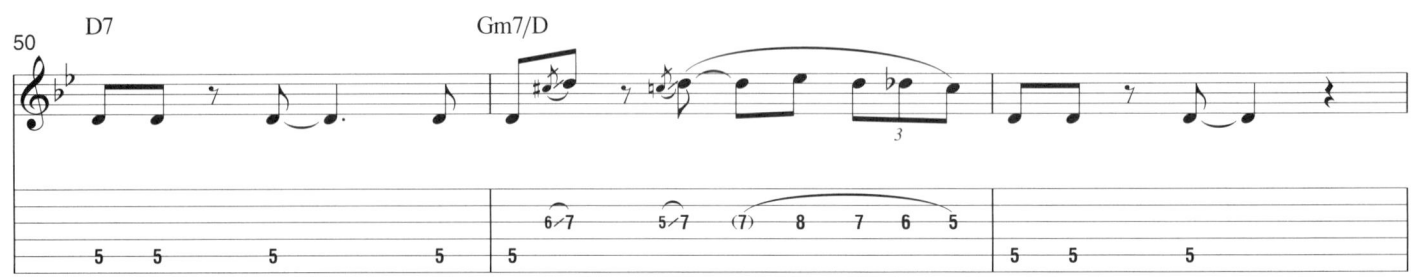
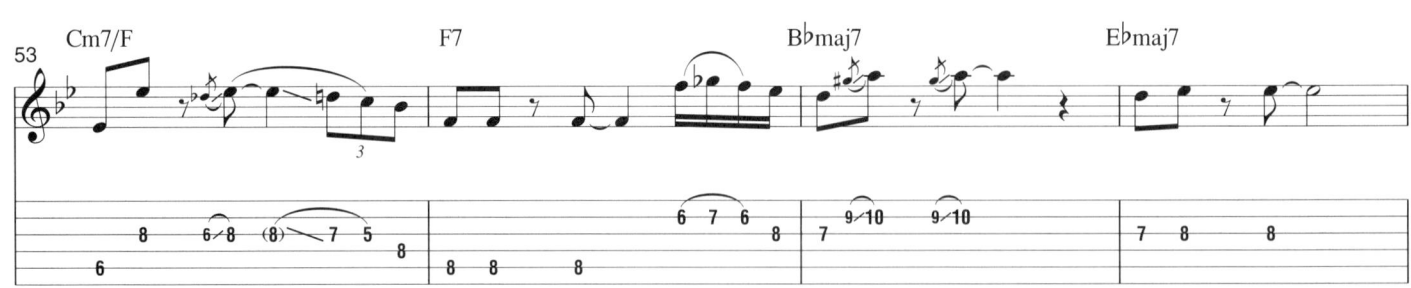

Eb7
Am7b5
D7
Db7
Solo 2nd Chorus 1:38
Cm7
F7
Bbmaj7
Bb7
Ebmaj7
Am7b5
D7
Gm7
G7
Cm7
F7
Bbmaj7
Ebmaj7
steady gliss.
Am7b5
D7#9
Gm7

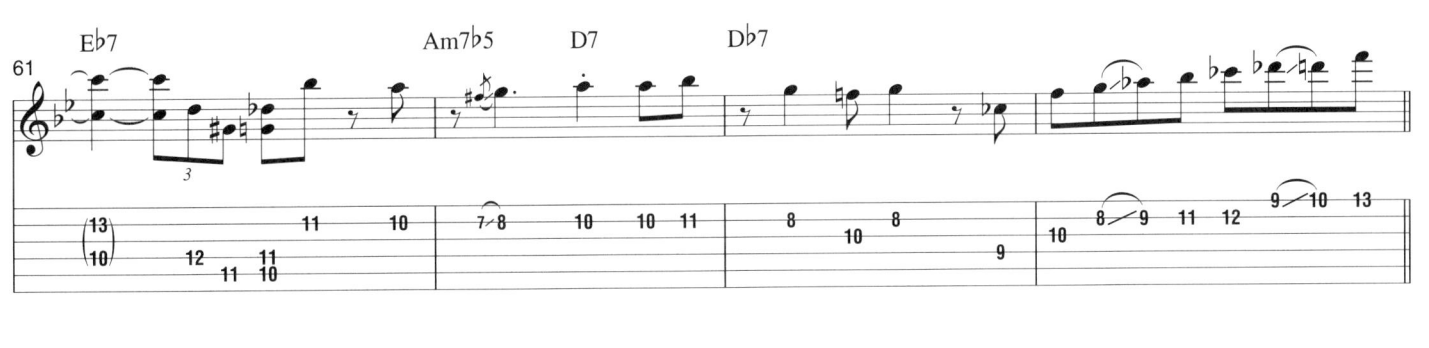

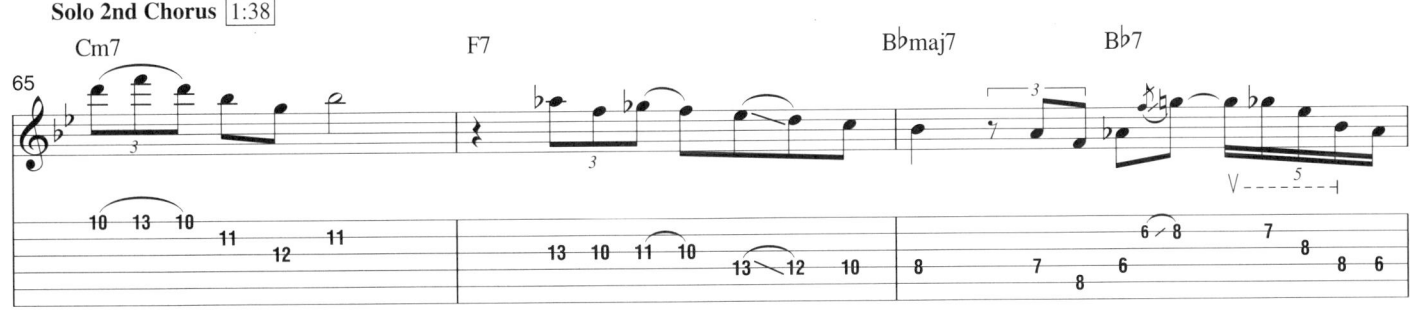

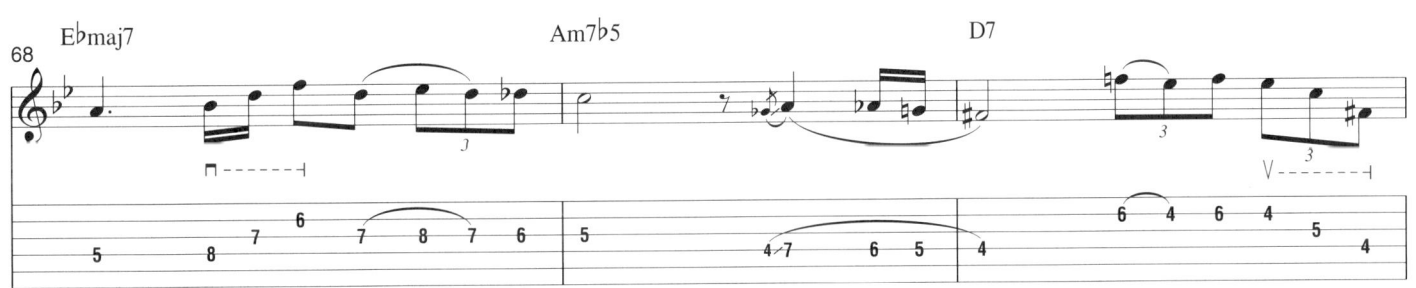

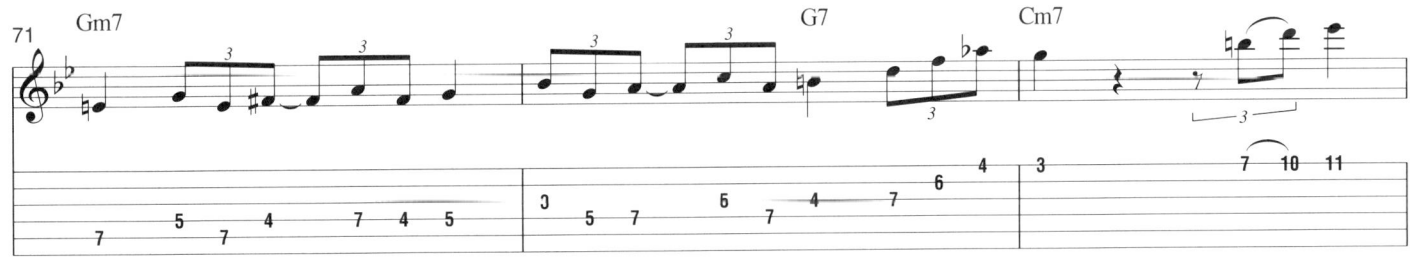

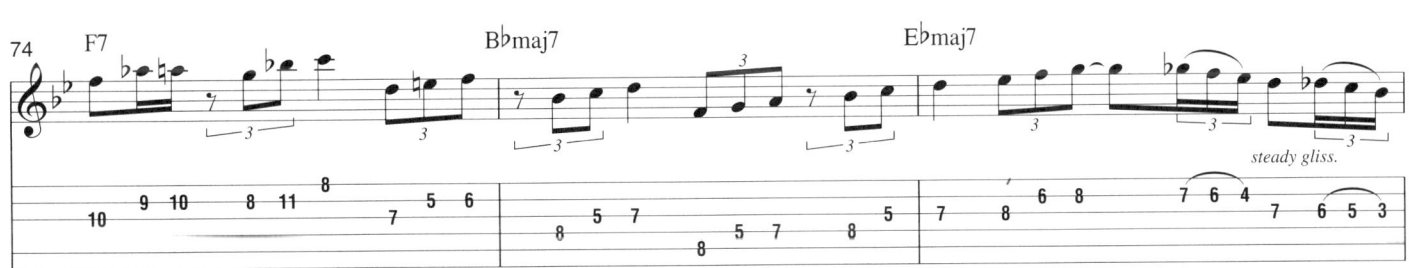

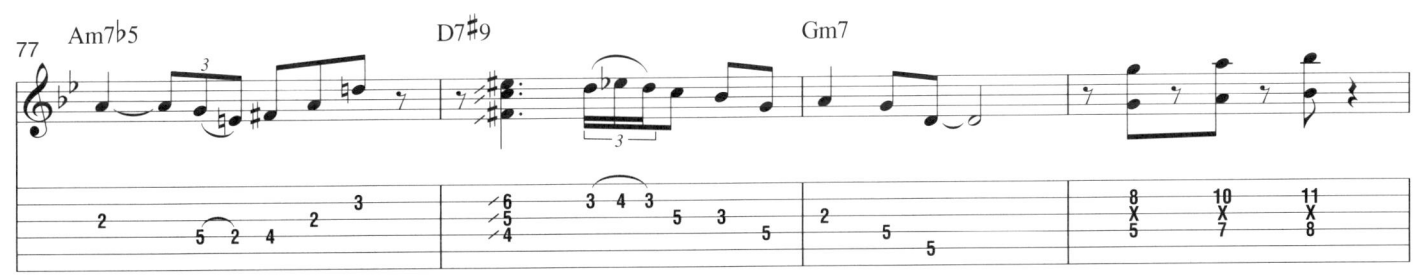

BIG BLUES
(*All Across the City*, 1989)
By James S. Hall

Figure 5—Intro, Head, and Solo

In the 1980s, as guitar virtuosity reached frenzied new heights, Hall remained a warm and thoughtful improviser. One of his finest records of that era is *All Across the City*, featuring his exquisitely sensitive quartet of pianist Gil Goldstein, bassist Steve La Spina, and drummer Terry Clarke. A modern take on the classic 12-bar form, the original composition "Big Blues" is a tribute to tenor saxophonist Stanley Turrentine, who, like Hall, was an enemy of the superfluous.

Hall kicks things off with a 16-bar intro, toying with pairs of Fs in two different octaves—along with lots of space—while the rhythm section gets into the groove. Hall's head begins in bar 17. The harmony is wide open; it's essentially based on one big F7 chord, which facilitates numerous substitutions and alterations. Also, dig the cool chromatic turnaround in the ninth and tenth bars of the form (A♭7–G7–G♭7; bars 25–26).

Hall plays the head twice, the second time (bars 29–40) in a higher octave. The melody is based, appropriately enough, on the F blues scale (F–A♭–B♭–C♭–C–E♭), stated in three four-bar phrases. Again, note the judicious use of space; for example, the ample breathing room at the end of each phrase.

Hall sticks pretty closely to the head during his first solo chorus, which begins in bar 41. Then, in bar 50, he takes things outside. As the rhythm section is playing with harmonic looseness here, Hall is most likely thinking not in relation to the turnaround but in relation to the F7 home chord. So, in the first half of bar 50, he plays a G♭ triad (G♭–B♭–D♭), which includes the ♭9 (G♭) and ♭13 (D♭) of F7. Similarly, in bar 51, Hall hits these tense notes, as well as the ♯11 (B).

In the last bar of his first chorus (bar 52), Hall sets up a rhythmic motif that he carries into his second chorus, culminating, in bar 54, with the ♭9 played way up the neck (14th-fret G♭). After a bar of rest, Hall releases tension by hitting the root (13th-fret F), followed by a series of supremely bluesy lines. In bars 61–62, Hall plays a neat trick with broken octaves: he slides down into each lower note from a pitch within the blues scale.

Hall plays a similar sliding idea in his third chorus, this time using assorted intervals as opposed to only octaves. In bar 69, he plays a high G, then lands on a note (A♭) that's a major 7th lower; in bar 70, he spans an octave (F to F); and in bar 71, a major 6th (C down to E♭). Beginning in bar 73, Hall plays another outside phrase by stringing together pairs of major and minor 3rds. In the second half of bar 73, note the half-step movement between the C–E♭ and D–C♭ note pairs.

In his fourth chorus, beginning in bar 77, Hall develops a motif similar to one played by saxophonist John Coltrane in his classic "A Love Supreme" solo. Hall hits some choice alterations here—the ♯9 (G♯/A♭) and ♭13 (D♭) in various octaves. Then, in bars 85–86, he plays an ultra-hip sequence, beginning with an A♭ arpeggio on the A♭7 chord. The shape is moved down a whole step in bar 85, then another whole step in bar 86, followed by a half step, bringing out the ♭9th and 13th of the G7 and G♭7 chords (respectively, A♭/G♯ and E; A♭♭/G and E♭).

Hall uses this same polychordal idea in his fifth chorus (bar 93), playing a G triad (G–B–D) over the IV chord, B♭7, and hitting the ♭9 (C♭/B) and 13 (G). In bar 97, as he did in previous choruses, Hall wraps things up with some outside lines. Note the chromatically descending B♭–A–A♭ line in bar 97, and the G♭–F–E line in bar 98. In the last two bars, Hall hits some more select alterations—the ♭13 (D♭) in bar 99 and the ♭9 (G♭) in bar 100.

Hall's sixth and final chorus is his most straightforwardly soulful, drawn mostly from the F blues scale—check out the expressive bends in bars 103 and 104. Dig also the chromatically descending major 6ths in bars 111–112, as well as the dyad—E♭–A♭, implying an F7♯9 chord (F–A–C–E♭–G♯/A♭)—with which Hall closes things out.

*Chord symbols reflect basic harmony.

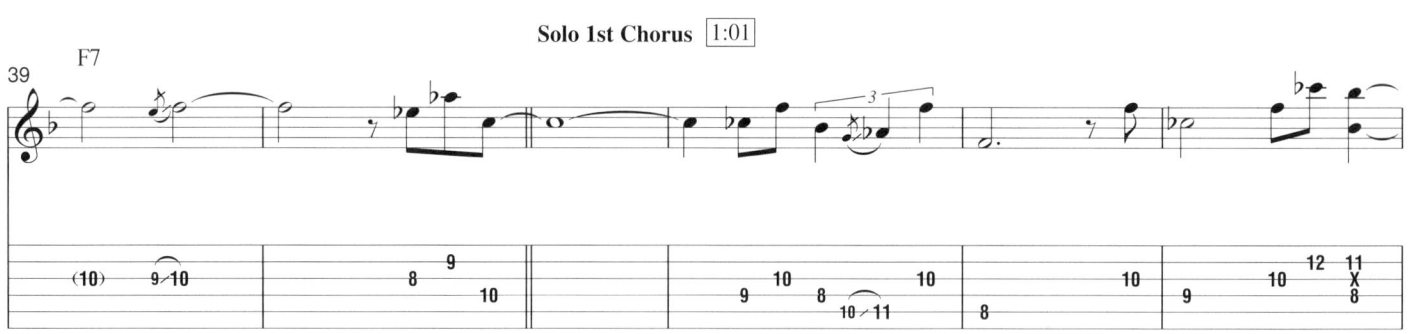
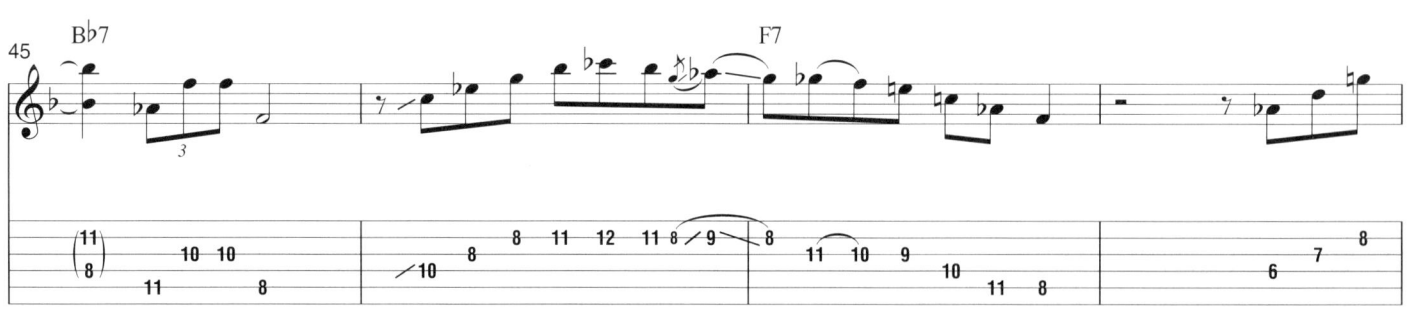
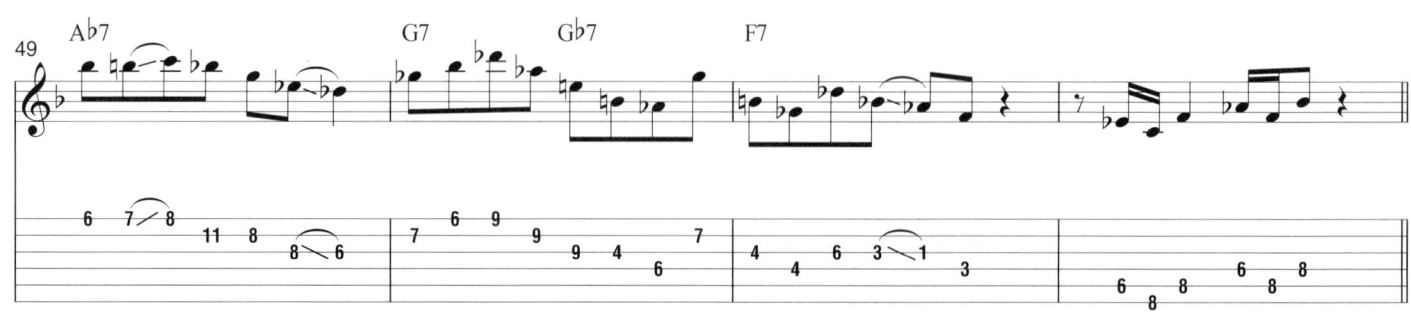

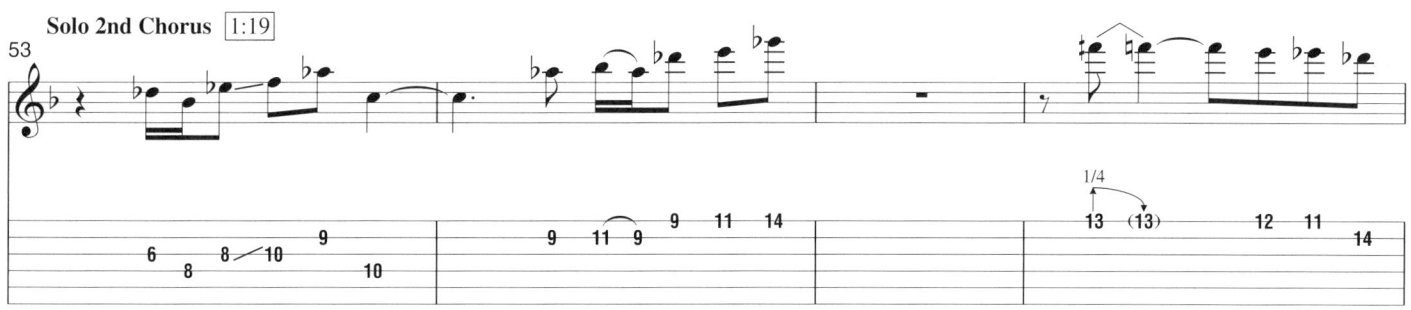
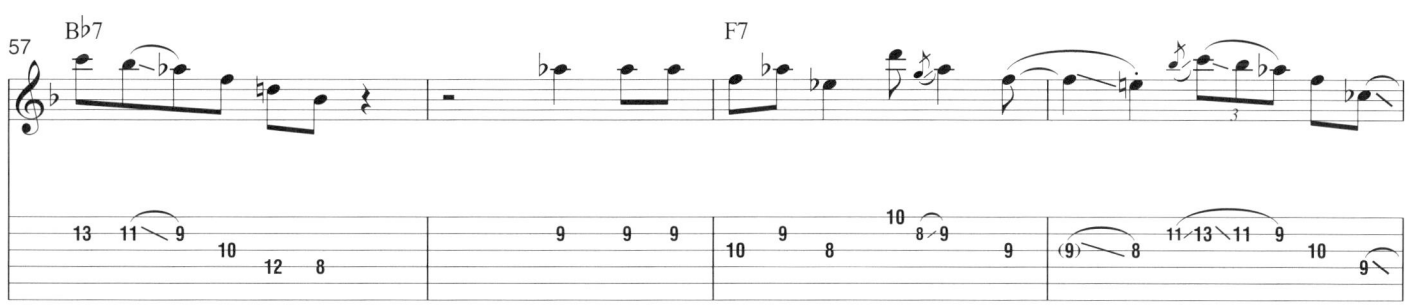
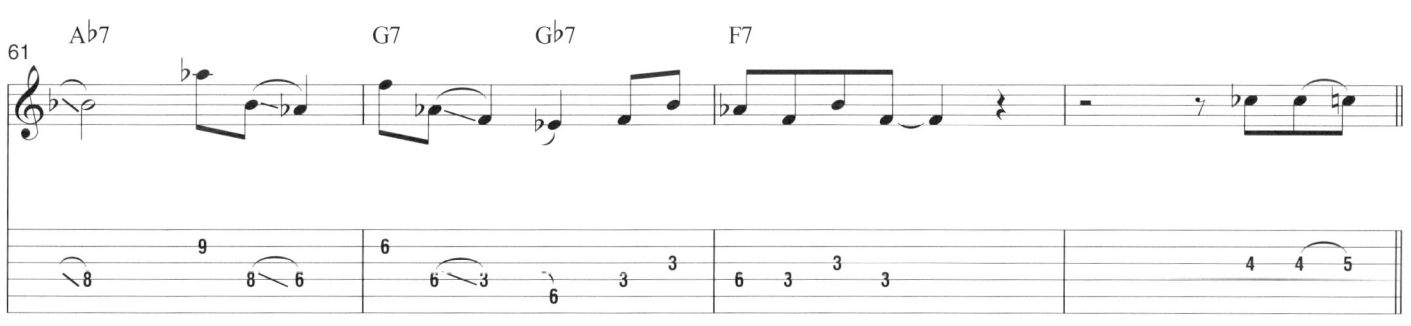
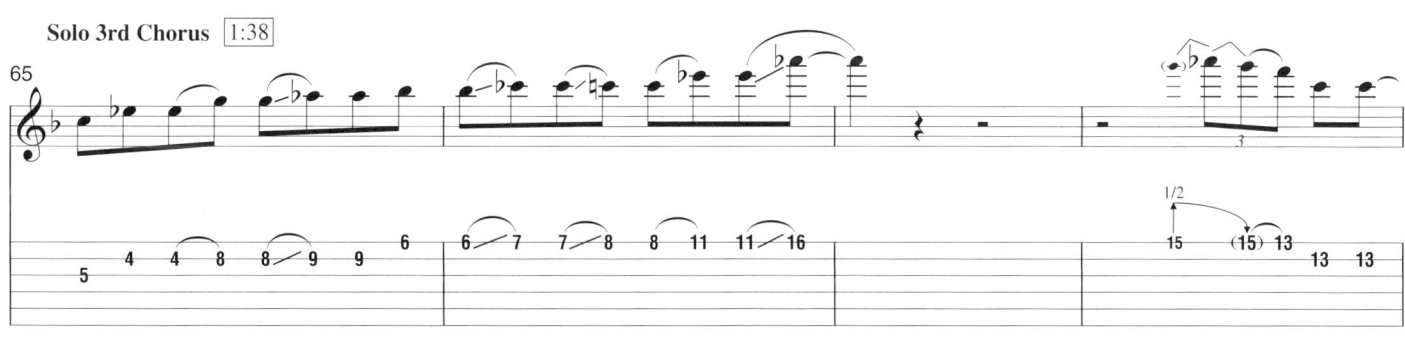
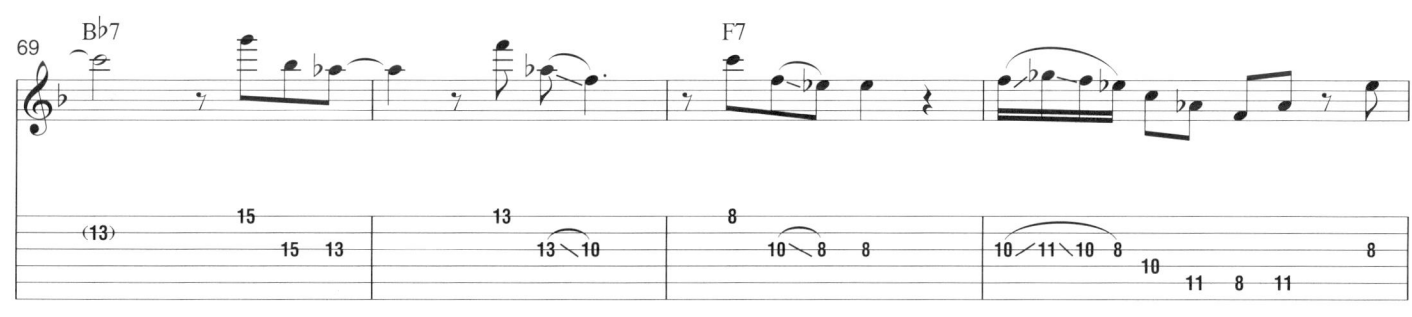

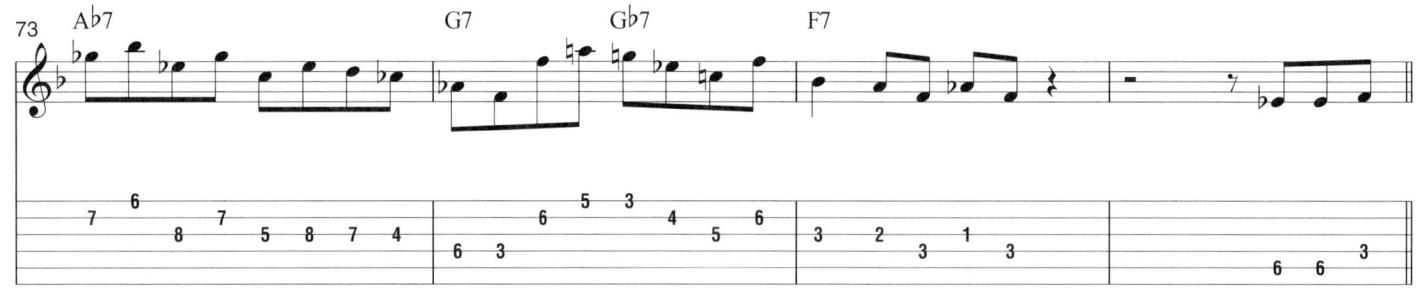

Solo 4th Chorus [1:56]

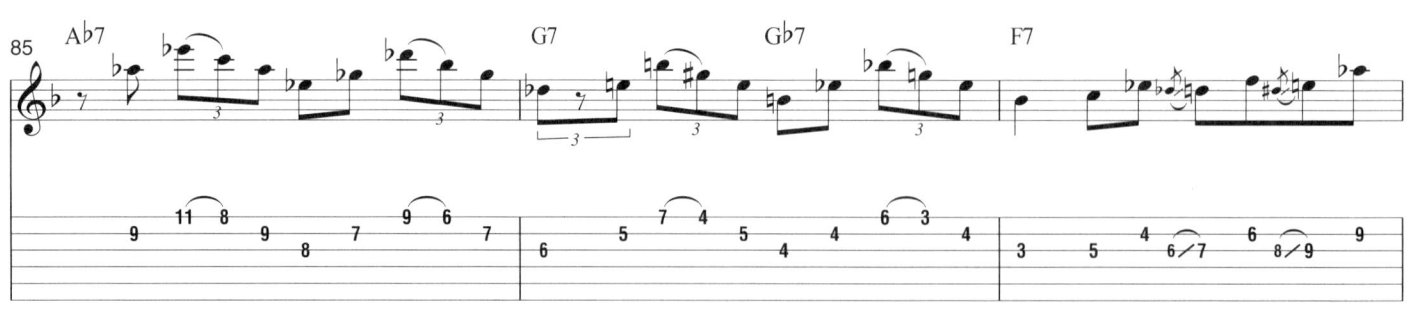

Solo 5th Chorus [2:15]

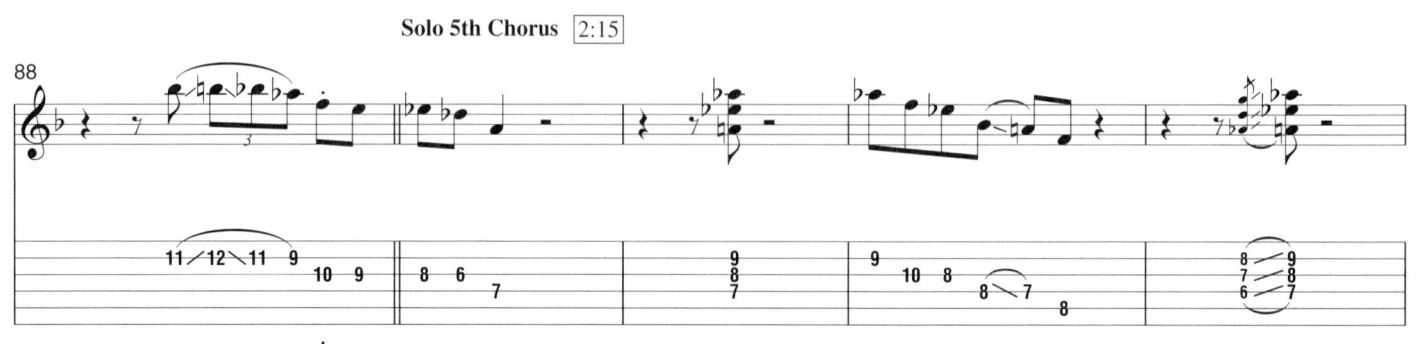

Figure 6—Interlude

Following La Spina's bass solo, Hall plays a hip interlude, which modulates up a major 3rd to the key of A major. Here, the guitarist—supported only by Clarke—improvises on two 12-bar blues choruses. He starts in bars 1–3 on the I chord (A7), with some lines within the fifth-position A minor pentatonic (A–C–D–E–G) box, before venturing into some chordal territory. In bar 4, Hall approaches the IV chord (D7) chromatically with a parallel series of 13th chords: C13, C#13, and D13, voiced on strings 1–4. Likewise, he returns to the I chord with a G13–G#13–A13 change in bars 6–7. In bars 9–12, Hall etches out a basic descending progression of E7–D7–C7–B7 with some parallel 9th-chord shapes.

In his second pass at the blues form, starting in bar 13, Hall plays some interesting chord substitutions. In bar 14, for instance, in place of the I chord, he plays Dm6 (voiced D–B–F–A) and F#7#9 (C#–A#–E–A) chords. Notice the smooth voice leading between the two chords: the highest note remains the same, while the bottom three notes descend by a half step. Another cool harmonic move occurs in bar 18: on beat 2, Hall plays an edgy D7#9#11 chord (voiced A–C–F–G#), which makes it way to a consonant C#m11 chord (F#–B–E–G#) on the "and" of beat 4, setting up a ii–V (C#m7–F#7) change in bars 19–20. Notice that Hall approaches the F#7 by a half step, from a G13 chord at the end of bar 19. In bar 25, the interlude modulates back to F major, and for eight bars Hall revisits the intro's octaves before ending the tune with a restatement of the head.

Fig. 6

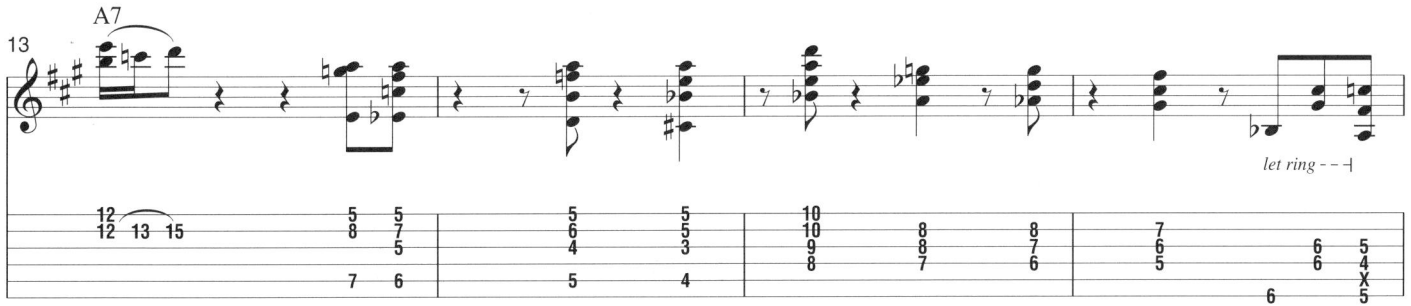
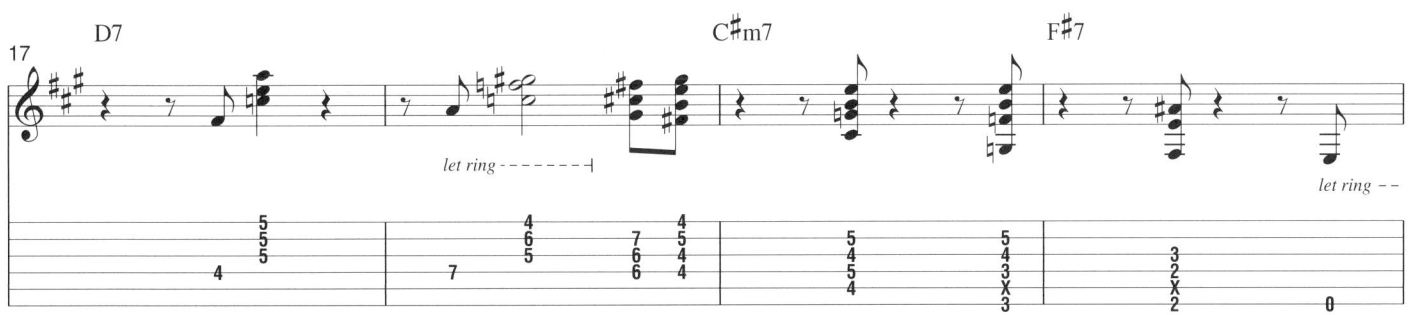
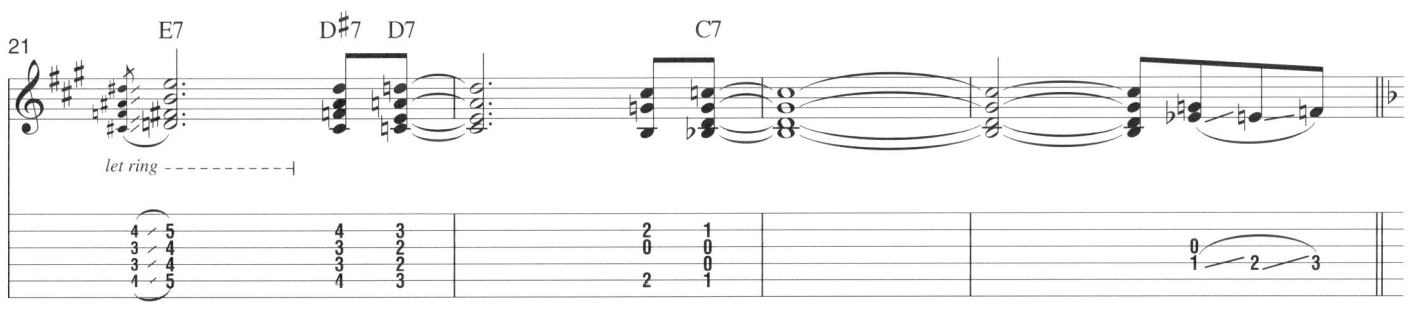
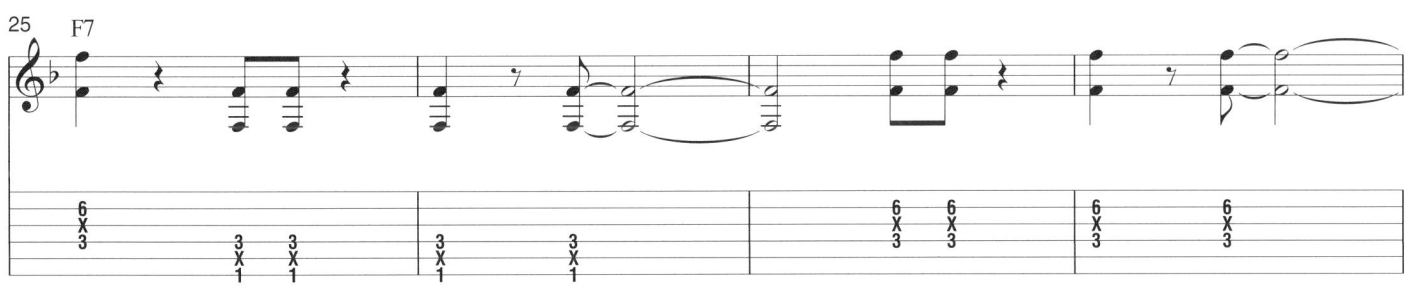
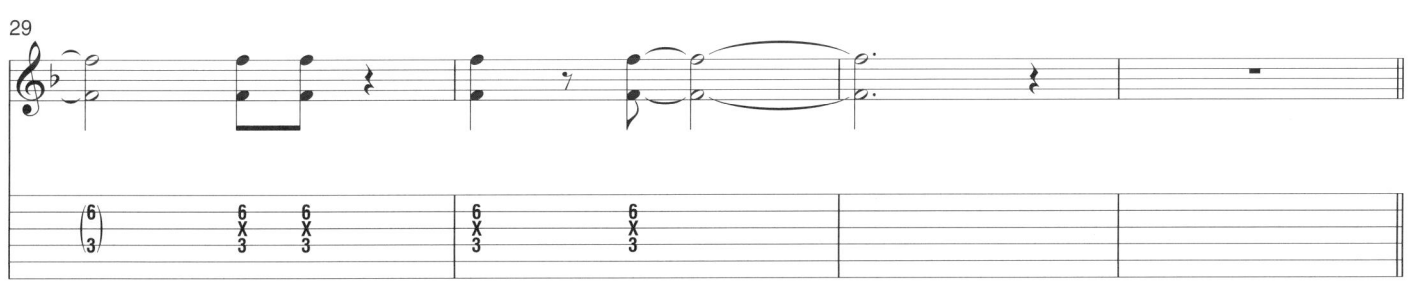

33

MY MAN'S GONE NOW
from PORGY AND BESS
(*Intermodulation*, 1966)
By George Gershwin, Du Bose and Dorothy Heyward and Ira Gershwin

Figure 7—Solo 1

As with saxophonist Sonny Rollins and bassist Ron Carter, Hall had an uncommonly strong musical chemistry with pianist Bill Evans. Hall and Evans recorded two duet albums, *Undercurrent* (1962) and *Intermodulation* (1966). Not only do these rank among the highlights of their respective catalogues, they are two of the greatest jazz recordings ever made.

One of the most memorable performances from either album is a thoughtful interpretation of "My Man's Gone Now," from the George and Ira Gershwin opera *Porgy and Bess* (1935). Played in the key of E minor in waltz time, the song has an unconventional AAB form, in which each section is 11 bars long. After an impressionistic four-bar intro by both players, Evans takes the melody while Hall lays down some gorgeous chords. Then, the guitarist takes a gloriously melodic solo, played entirely in single notes. While he draws largely from the E natural minor scale (E–F#–G–A–B–C–D) in the A-section, Hall keeps things interesting by mixing up his note values, using quarter, half, and sixteenth notes in the first few bars alone. He also employs various intervallic strategies, such as the descending series of perfect 4ths in bar 3. Then there's the blues element: in bar 12, for example, Hall plays an earthy phrase that comes straight from the E minor pentatonic scale (E–G–A–B–D).

In the B-section, with its ascending series of ii–V progressions (Bb13–Eb6/9, B13–Em9, C#+7–F#m9), Hall selects notes that clearly outline the changes. Particularly rich is his handling of the C#+7 chord in bar 27, where he approaches the chord from a half step above before smoothly landing on the 3rd (A) of the subsequent F#m9 chord from a whole step above. Hall begins closing out his solo in bar 30 by cleverly playing notes from a G triad (G–B–D) over the Em9 chord. Over the next few bars, he repeatedly pulls off to the open E string; this offers nice timbral contrast to the other notes, which are fretted in seventh position. After outlining the B+7 chord in bar 33, Hall concludes his solo simply, ending on the open sixth string in the first bar of Evans's solo.

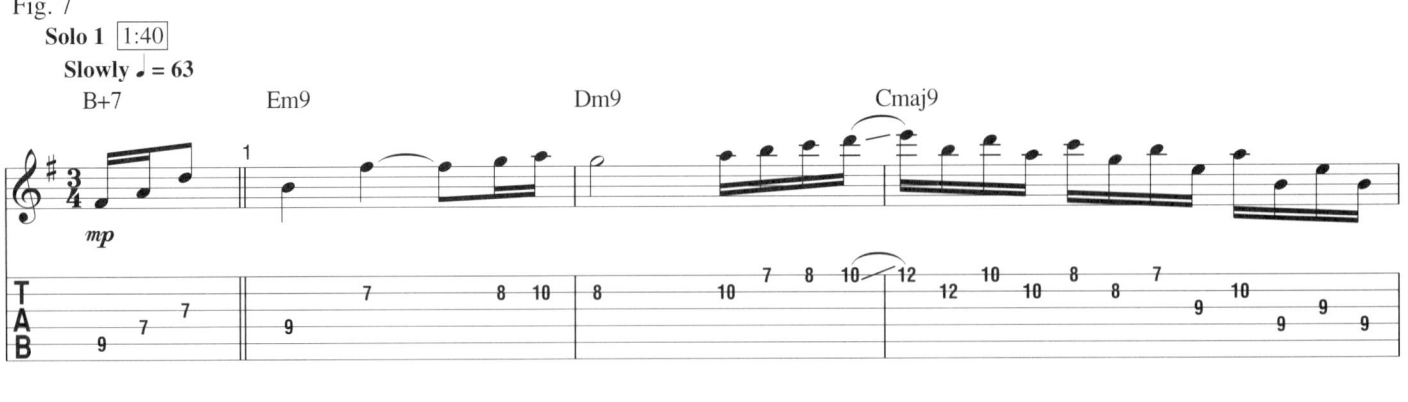

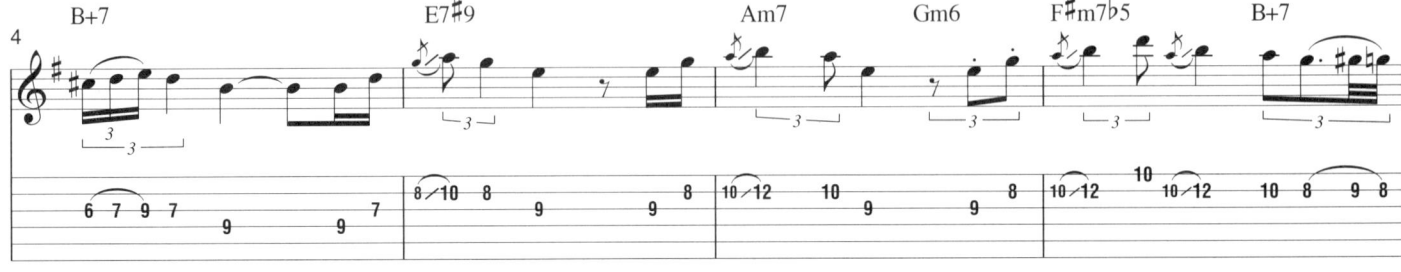

© 1935 (Renewed 1962) GEORGE GERSHWIN MUSIC, IRA GERSHWIN MUSIC and DU BOSE AND DOROTHY HEYWARD MEMORIAL FUND
All Rights Administered by WB MUSIC CORP.
All Rights Reserved   Used by Permission

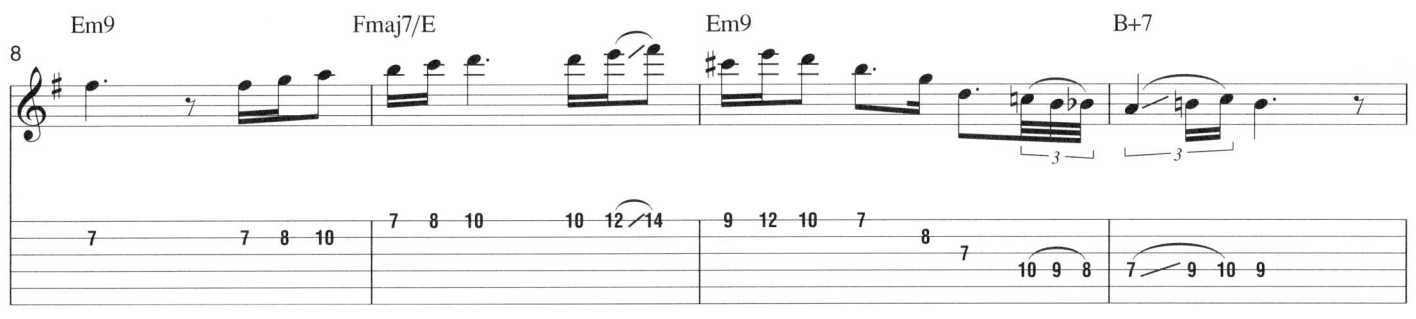
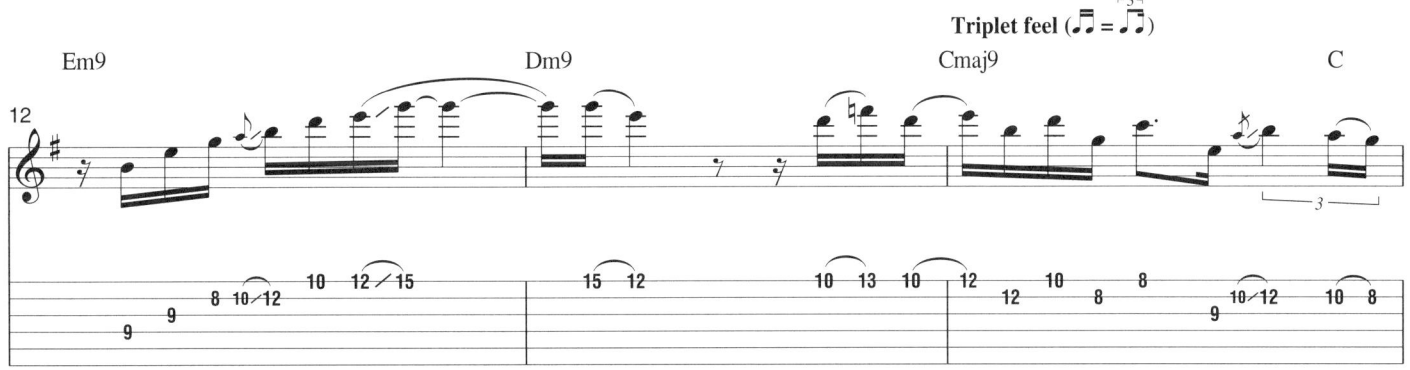
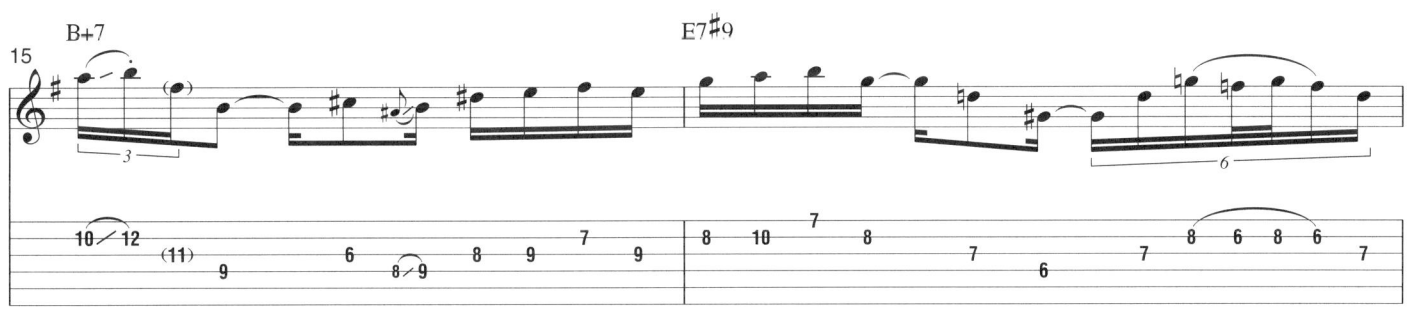
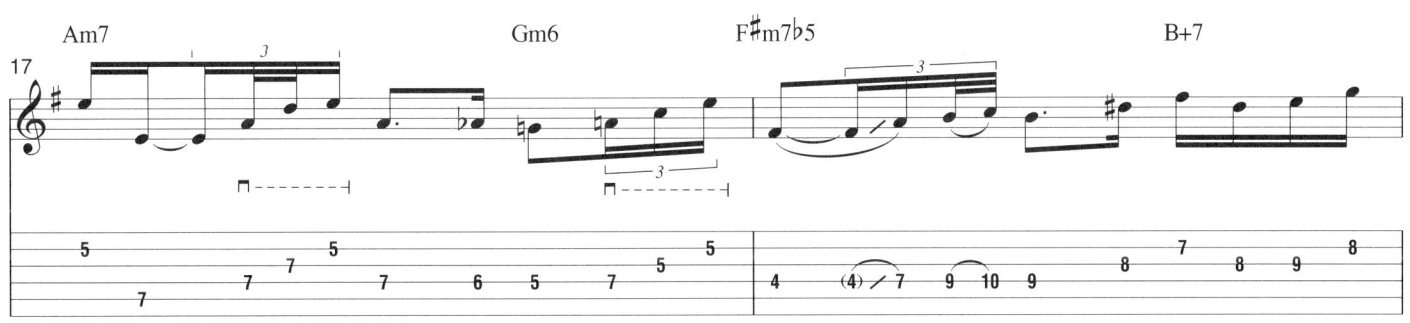
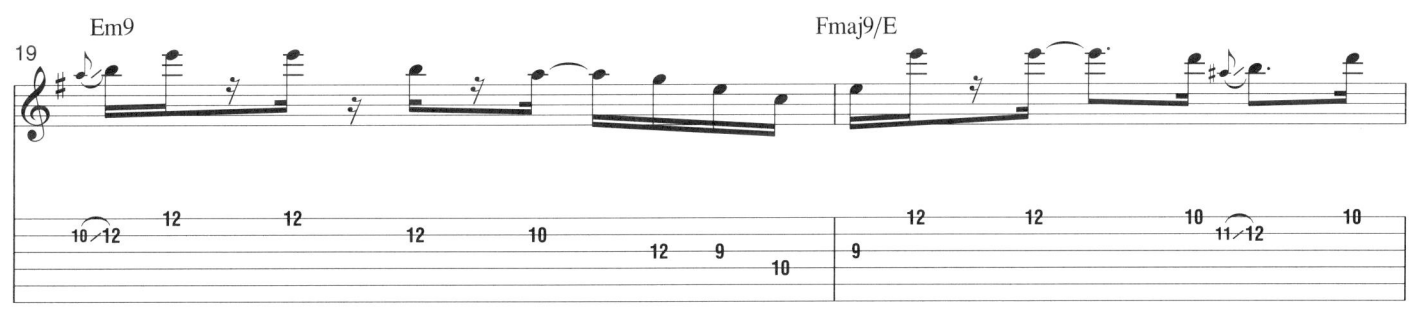

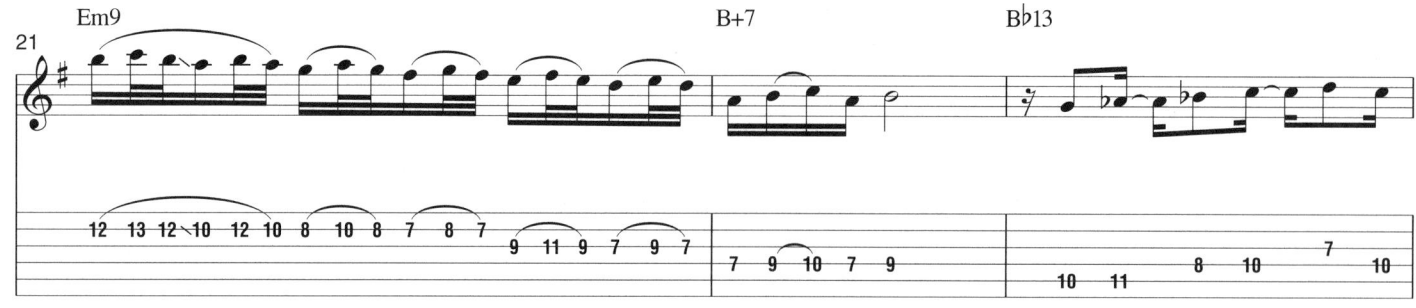
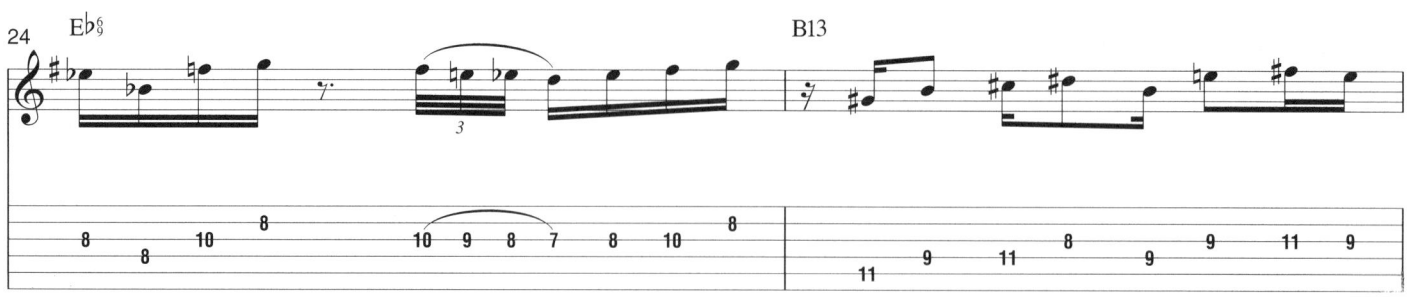
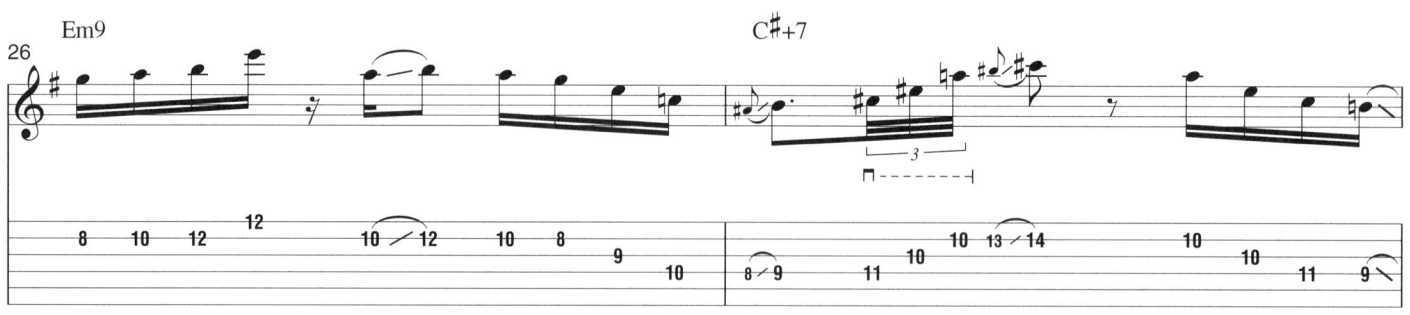
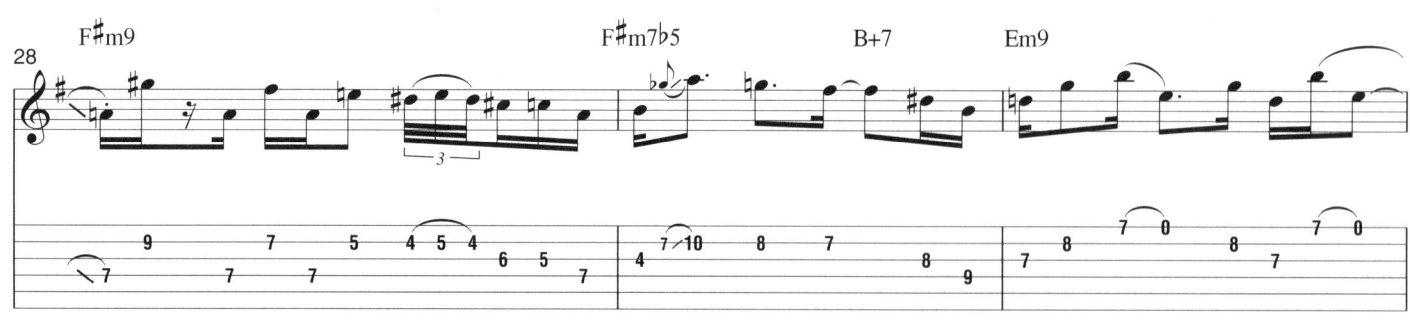

36

Figure 8—Solo 2

In the A-sections of his second solo, Hall sticks more closely to the original melody, embellishing it here and there with soulful, whole-step slides. If you listen to each slide carefully, you can hear a chromatic pitch in between the lower note and its target pitch. Bars 6, 17, and 18 are rife with slurred chromatic passing tones, a hallmark of Hall's ballad style. In bar 20, Hall reacts to Evans's 3rd-based comping by playing an attractive series of harmonic 3rds, yielding, in bar 23, to four-note block chords that are broken up in a syncopated manner. Colorful chord clusters appear in bar 30. Here, Hall pits fretted notes from the E natural minor scale on strings 2 and 3 against the ringing open first string, resulting in some rich but delicate sounds—particularly the voicings that contain both an open E and a fretted E. The solo is closed out with a sonorous, six-note Em9 chord, strummed with a reverse rake.

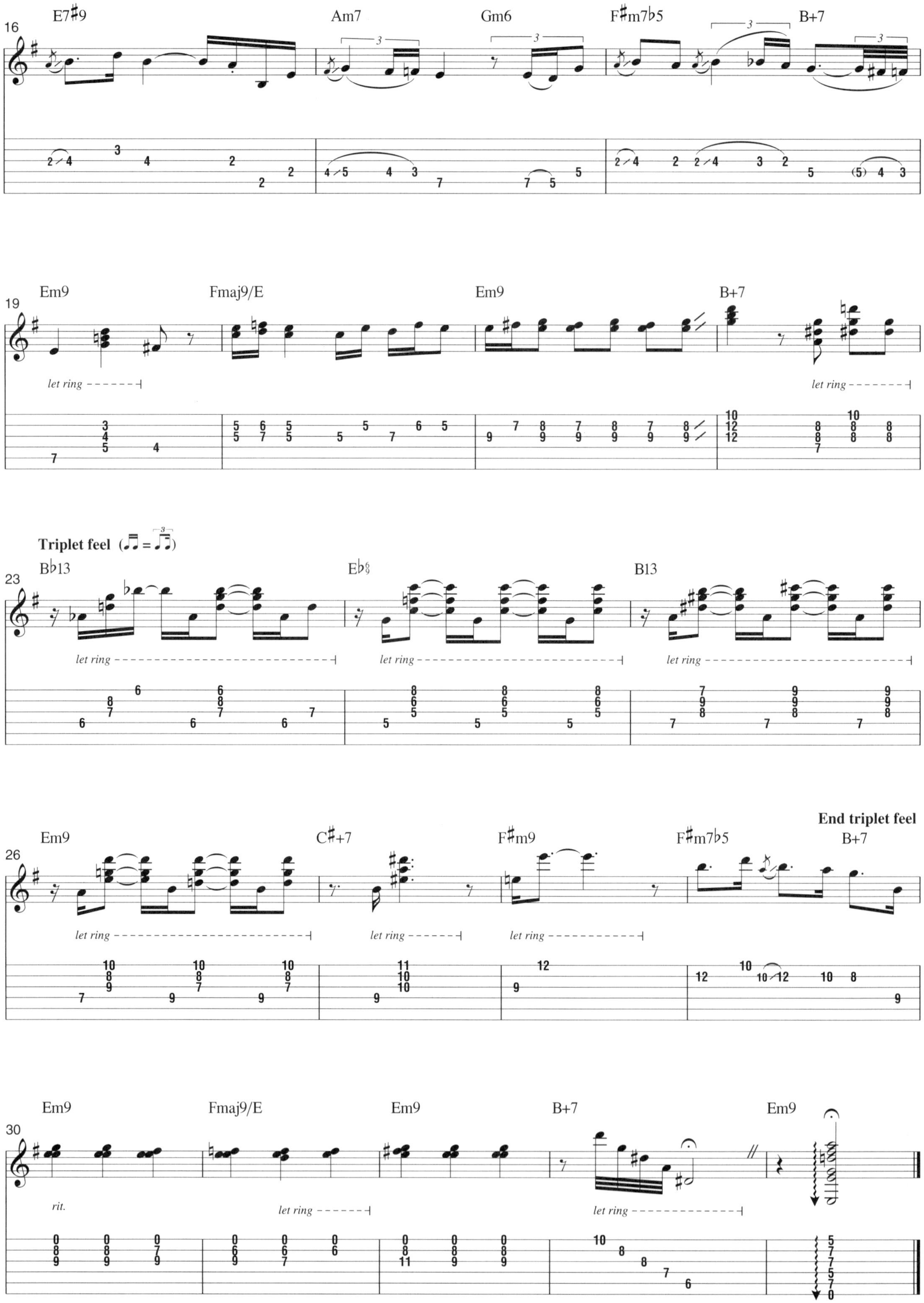
E7♯9
Am7
Gm6
F♯m7♭5
B+7
Em9
Fmaj9/E
Em9
B+7
let ring
let ring
Triplet feel
B♭13
E♭6/9
B13
let ring
let ring
let ring
End triplet feel
Em9
C♯+7
F♯m9
F♯m7♭5
B+7
let ring
let ring
let ring
Em9
Fmaj9/E
Em9
B+7
Em9
rit.
let ring
let ring

PRELUDE TO A KISS
(*Ballad Essentials*, 2000)

Words by Irving Gordon and Irving Mills
Music by Duke Ellington

Figure 9—Head

One of jazz's most lyrical guitarists, Hall has a special way with the ballad—the perfect vehicle for his warm, rich tone; melodic and harmonic inventiveness; and horn-like articulations. Hall's gentler side is perhaps best witnessed on *Ballad Essentials*, an excellent compilation of the guitarist's recordings for the Concord Jazz label.

Originally appearing on *All Across the City* (1989), "Prelude to a Kiss" offers a terrific representation of Hall's ballad style. The guitarist plays this Duke Ellington classic with pianist Gil Goldstein, bassist Steve La Spina, and drummer Terry Clarke, all of whom give particularly sensitive support. The tune is based on the standard 32-bar AABA form; the A-sections are in C major; the bridge, in E. During the head, Hall is rather liberal in his reading of the melody; for example, in its original version, bar 3 contained the chromatically descending G♯–G–F♯–F line in straight quarter notes. But Hall, using eighth-note triplets, adds notes a 3rd above or below the original melody, save for on the F♯. In the interest of coherence, a similar invention can be found in bars 11 and 27, and bars 9, 19, and 24 contain comparable rhythmic motifs.

In bar 6, Hall adds pitches from an Am7 arpeggio (A–C–E–G) to connect the original melody notes C (string 4, fret 10) and D (string 1, fret 10), then moves from D to the next original melody note, C (string 1, fret 8), via chromatic pull-offs and a slide, sounding much like a horn player. Hall adds another Am7 arpeggio in bar 14, and similar chromatics can be found in bar 18, albeit played in an ascending manner.

Not only does the head reveal Hall's melodic and harmonic sophistication, it also shows his bluesy side: check out the subtle, half-step bends in bars 16 and 26, as well as the soulful, grace-note slides (from A to B) in bar 30.

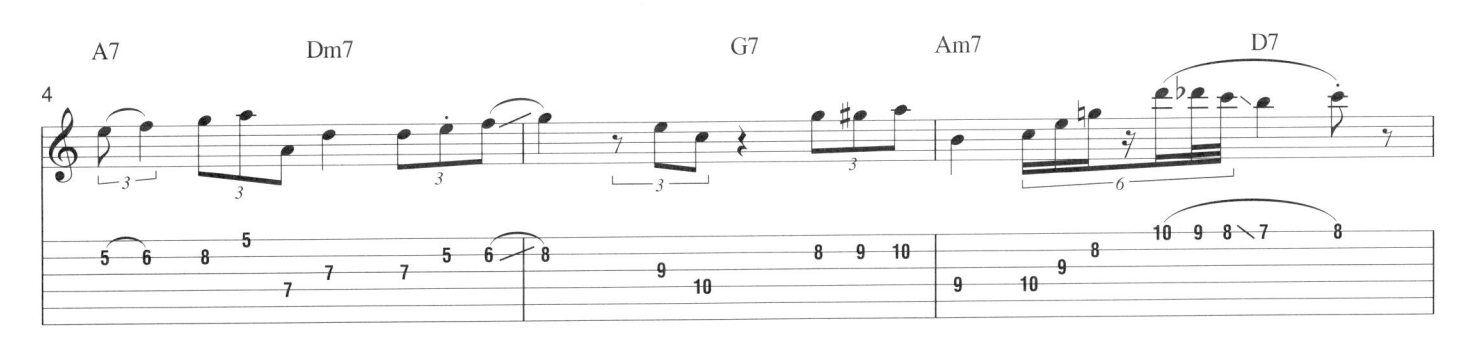

7 Dm7 G7 Cmaj7 Em7 A7 D7 G7
10 C7 Fmaj7 B7 E7 A7 Dm7
13 G7 Am7 D7 Dm7 G7
16 Cmaj7 F#m7 B7 Emaj7 C#m7 F#m7 B7
19 Emaj7 C#m7 F#m7 B7 Emaj7 C#m7

Figure 10—Solo and Outro

Hall begins his solo at the B-section, playing nicely syncopated lines from the E major scale (E–F#–G#–A–B–C#–D#) in bar 1, and adding chromatics in bars 2 and 3—he starts off with the root (B) of the B7 chord and travels up the neck in half steps until he hits the 7th (D#) of the Emaj7 chord. Beginning in bar 3, Hall plays some nice, descending 3rd slides, bringing out the 7th and 5th (B) of Emaj7, the b7th (B) and 5th (G#) of C#m7, and the 9th (G#) and b7th (E) of F#m7.

In bar 5, Hall, using some of the same chromatic embellishments as in the head, plays the original melody. Then, he works a sixteenth-note rhythmic motif throughout bars 7 and 8, hitting some choice notes: the #9 (F##/G) and 9 (F#) on the E7 chord, and the b9 (Bb) on A7. In bar 8, Hall plays an interesting variation on Ellington's straight-quarter-note melody: he delays the original notes by half a beat, approaching each one from a major 3rd above, on the same string.

Following a bluesy half-step bend in bar 9, Hall works some more 3rds—mostly minor—this time falling underneath the original melody notes in a triplet-based, eighth-note rhythm. He ends his solo in much the same way he played the head: adding some chromatic slurs (bar 10) and an Am7 arpeggio (bar 14).

The outro begins at bar 16—and things get very interesting. In bars 18–21, over a C pedal tone, Hall quotes from Ellington's "Mood Indigo," harmonizing it mainly with parallel triads and dominant 9th voicings for a strikingly modern effect. Then, as the C pedal continues in bar 22, Hall re-harmonizes "Prelude to a Kiss," beginning with parallel half-diminished 7th chords and settling in on a D♭maj9 chord (voiced D♭–E♭–A♭–C) in bars 23–25. On beat 4 of bar 25, he plays an ultra-tense A13♭9♯11 chord (G–B♭–D♯–F♯), still over the C pedal, and moves it around chord-melody style through bar 29.

In bar 30, Hall begins to close things up with a sixteenth-note line based closely on the original melody, with contracted harmonic rhythms. An interesting detail is found at the end of bar 31 where Hall implies a G7♭9 chord (G–B–D–F–A♭) with just the sixth-fret A♭ and the open G string. Beginning in bar 33, Hall plays another altered voicing in descending half steps, finally coming to rest on a wistful C6/9add♯11 chord.

15 Full Band

16 Slow Demo meas. 1-35

Fig. 10

Solo 2:36

A7
Dm7
G7
Am7
D7
Dm7
G7
Cmaj7
Outro 3:32
let ring
D7
G7
C7
Fmaj7
Free time
B7
E7
A7
Dm7
G7♭9
rit.
let ring
Am7
F♯m11♭5
G9sus4
let ring
let ring
G7♭5
C6/9
C6/9add♯11

SCRAPPLE FROM THE APPLE
(*Jim Hall Live!*, 1976)
By Charlie Parker

Figure 11—Intro and Head

As evidenced on "Angel Eyes" (see page 12), from *Jim Hall Live!*, Hall is known to really stretch out at club dates. The guitarist's reading of saxophonist Charlie Parker's "Scrapple From the Apple" comes from the same set of 1975 dates at Toronto's Bourbon Street, with bassist Don Thompson and drummer Terry Clarke. On the tune, Hall improvises some rarified ideas in some of his most fearsome choruses ever recorded.

In the 16-bar intro, while Thompson holds down a C pedal tone, Hall plays syncopated Fsus2 (F–G–C) and A♭sus2 (A♭–B♭–E♭) chords, implying a big C7♭9♭13 chord (C–E–G–B♭–D♭–A♭). Then, Hall takes the head, which is based on "Rhythm Changes"—the chord progression of George and Ira Gershwin's "I Got Rhythm," with its 32-bar AABA form, the bridge of which circles through a series of dominant 7th chords (A7, D7, G7, and C7). In each A-section, Hall sticks closely to Parker's original lines, varying things a little in the last bar. The guitarist improvises his own phrases over the bridge (33–40), playing some wide leaps—such as the major 7th jump, from F to E, in bar 37—as well as some slippery chromatics, as seen on beat 1 of bar 39.

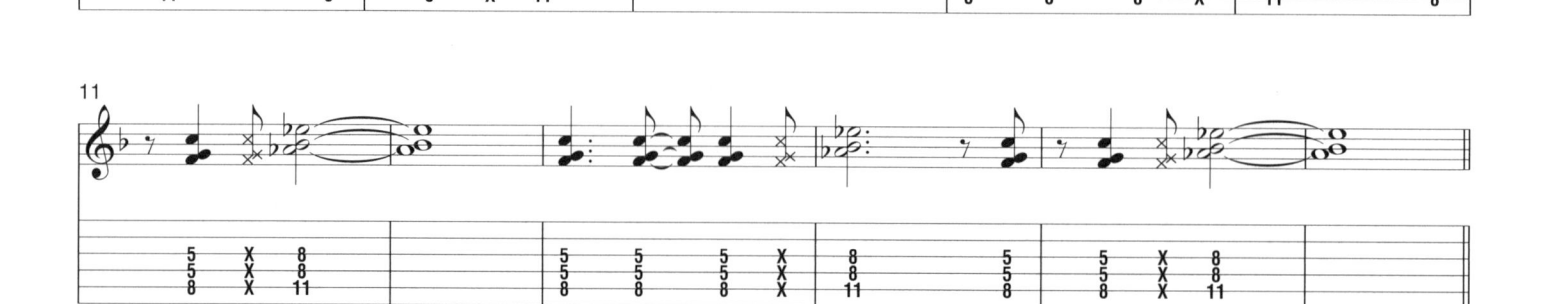

Copyright © 1957 (Renewed 1985) Atlantic Music Corp.
International Copyright Secured   All Rights Reserved

Head 0:18

Gm7
C7
Gm7
C7
Fmaj7
Gm7
C7
Fmaj7
Gm7
Am7
D7
Gm7
C7
Gm7
C7
Fmaj7
Gm7
C7
Fmaj7
Gm7
Fmaj7
A7
D7
G7
C7

Figure 12—Solo (Choruses 1 & 2)

Throughout his solo, Hall plays with harmonic freedom, as he is not bound by chordal accompaniment. So, in the first four bars, rather than outline the chords, he simply plays a phrase from the F major scale (F–G–A–Bb–C–D–E). And, in bar 5, instead of sticking to the original Fmaj7 chord, Hall plays notes that imply an altered F7 chord: the #9 (G#), b7 (Eb), and b9 (Gb). In bars 9–13, Hall plays a constant sixth-fret F, underneath which he syncopates a nifty chromatic line on string 3. This motif is developed in the next several bars, with additional notes on string 4. During the bridge, in bars 17–24, Hall negotiates the dominant cycle with a series of angular lines, the last note of which ends on a chord tone. For example, in bar 20, Hall lands on the 3rd (F#) of D7, and in bar 22, he lands on the b7th (F) of G7. The last A-section contains some more chromatics, such as the ascending C–Db–D–D#–E line in bars 25–26, and the sequence of non-diatonic perfect 4ths (G#–D# and F#–C#) in bar 29.

Chromaticism continues in the second chorus—check out the abundance of passing tones in the first several bars. Other highlights include parallel arpeggios; for example, the Cmaj7 and Cbmaj7 shapes of bar 39. Since Hall is viewing the A-section as one big F chord, as opposed to the original series of changes, Cbmaj7 brings out the b9th (Gb) and b5th (Cb) of an altered F7 chord. In the bridge, beginning in bar 49, Hall rakes and slides through some basic triads—G on the A7 chord and C on the D7—which are then answered by a descending chromatic line over the subsequent G7 and C7 chords. Hall wraps up the chorus with some lines drawn from the F major scale, with the addition of a few passing tones; note the rhythmic variations on the lone F note in the last several bars.

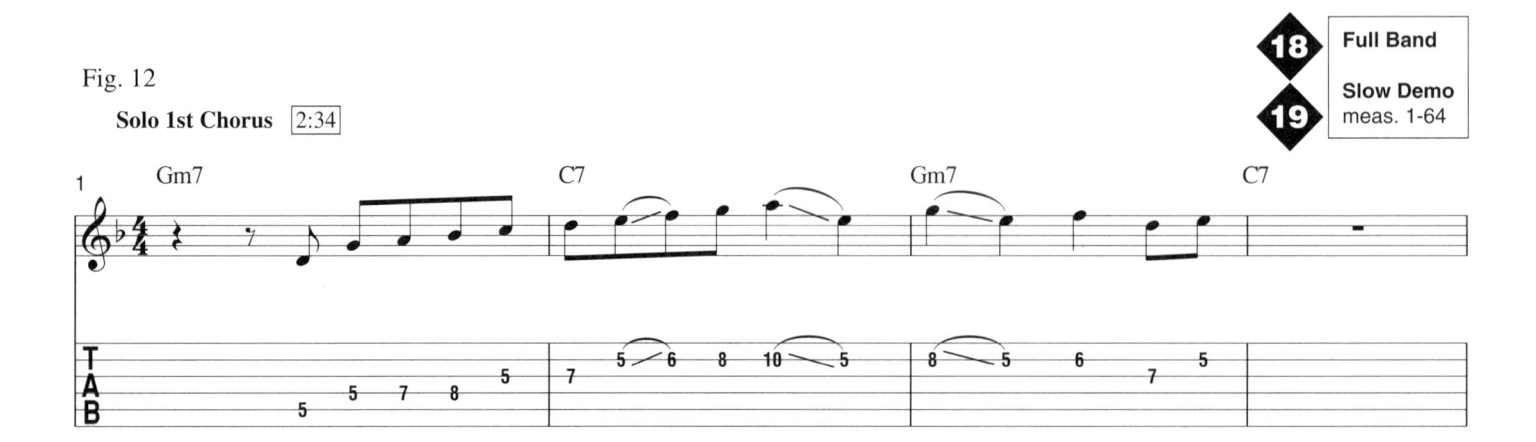

Fig. 12

Solo 1st Chorus 2:34

18 Full Band
19 Slow Demo meas. 1-64

5 Fmaj7 Gm7 C7 Fmaj7 Gm7 Am7 D7
9 Gm7 C7 Gm7 C7
13 Fmaj7 Gm7 C7 Fmaj7 Gm7 Fmaj7
17 A7 D7
21 G7 C7

Gm7 C7 Gm7 C7
Fmaj7 Gm7 C7 Fmaj7
Solo 2nd Chorus 3:07
Gm7 C7 Gm7 C7
Fmaj7 Gm7 C7 Fmaj7 Gm7 Am7 D7
Gm7 C7 Gm7 C7

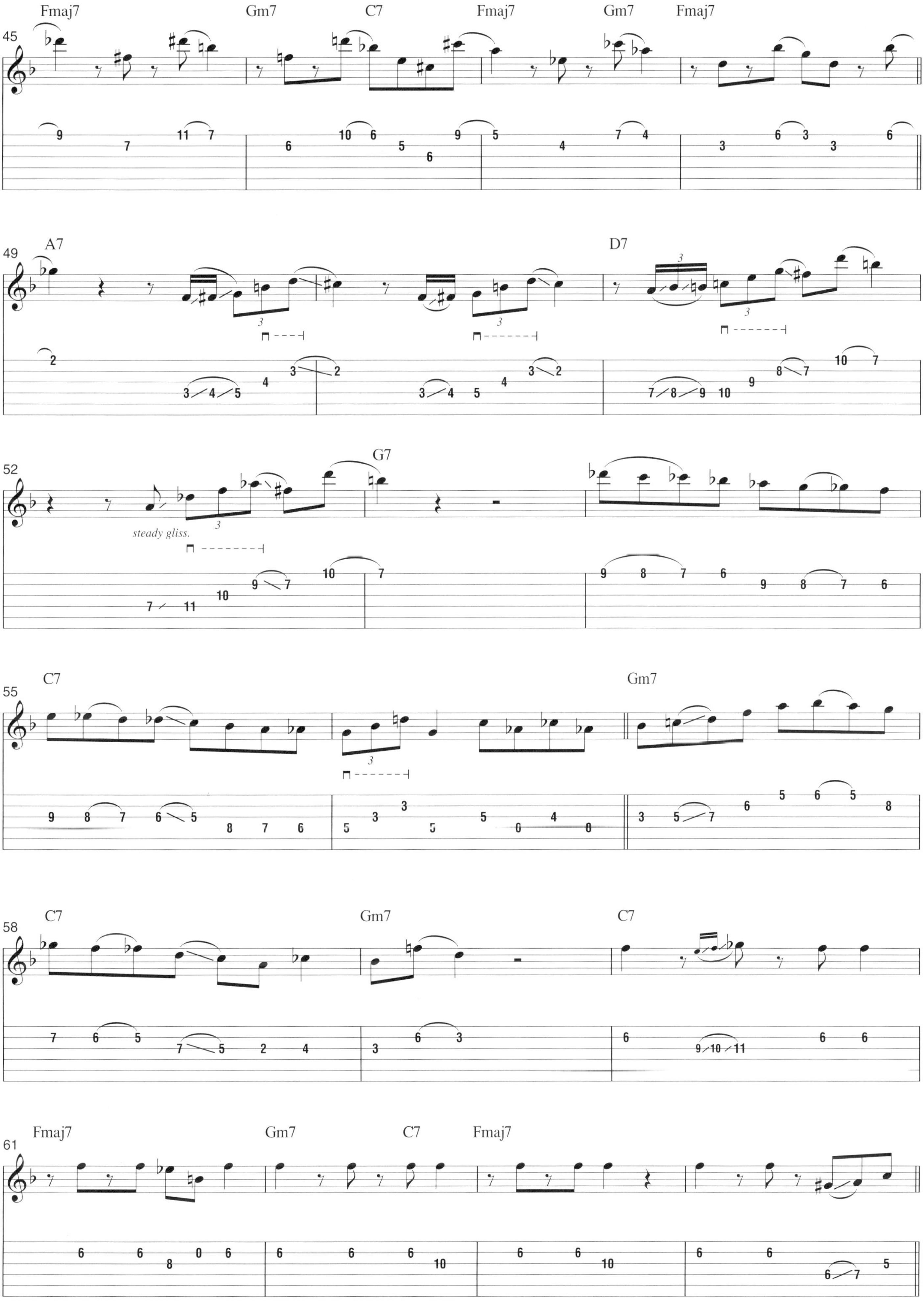
45
Fmaj7
Gm7
C7
Fmaj7
Gm7
Fmaj7
49
A7
D7
52
G7
steady gliss.
55
C7
Gm7
58
C7
Gm7
C7
61
Fmaj7
Gm7
C7
Fmaj7

ST. THOMAS
(*Alone Together*, 1972)
By Sonny Rollins

Figure 13—Head and Solo

From *Alone Together*, "St. Thomas" is one of the most well-known tunes of saxophone colossus Sonny Rollins. (It's also one of the most famous of all jazz standards.) Based on a traditional Caribbean tune, "St. Thomas" is played with a brisk Calypso feel. The melody is entirely in C major; the chords have some nice ii–V movement (Dm7–G7 and Em7–A7) throughout, as well as a hip turnaround (C–C/E–F–F#°–G) in the last four bars.

Hall begins the tune by stating the melody in single notes, and then switches to octaves in bar 9. Meanwhile, Carter plays a bass line that implies some non-diatonic 7th chords not found in the original composition: Bb7 in bar 9 and Ab7 in bar 11. After reverting to single notes at the end of bar 12, Hall ends the head with a neat chord move that involves contrary movement. He states the G7 chord with just two notes, the b7th (F) on bottom and the 3rd (B) on top. The B ascends by a half step, becoming the root (C) of the C chord, while the F descends by a half step, becoming the 3rd (E).

In his seven-chorus solo, Hall carefully develops several different ideas, seeing them to their logical conclusions. In the first chorus, he sticks closely to the original melody but adds palm-muting for textural contrast. He throws in some more octaves in bars 25–28, and ends the chorus with some playful rhythmic delay, anticipating each of the melody's final two notes with a quarter-note rest.

Another interesting textural device is used in the second chorus. Hall plays the open G string throughout, adding notes on string 4 to bring out the changes. The timbral contrast between the open string and the fifth-fret G is akin to that of the same note played with different fingerings on a saxophone. Most strikingly, Hall toys with some hip chromatic movement: in bars 41–44, against the open G, he plays a descending Bb–A–Ab–G line over the Em7–A7–Dm7–G7 progression; similarly, in bars 45–46, he uses the notes Bb, A, Ab, and G to connect the C/E, F, F#°, and G chords, respectively. Hall carries this idea throughout his third chorus.

In his fourth and fifth choruses, Hall changes things up by strumming some chords that are voiced on strings 2, 3, and 5; the 4th string is muted. This not only reduces sonic clutter, it makes for a nice percussive sound, a welcome quality given the lack of a drummer. For rhythmic support, Hall occasionally hits a low open string, or just the root of a chord, and at other times he mutes the strings altogether. Near the end of each of these choruses, he ties everything together by returning to the octave idea established during the head.

Hall builds excitement in his final two choruses by moving the three-note voicings up a set—to strings 1, 2, and 4—and strumming them in a similarly percussive manner. Note that Hall sometimes moves these voicings in a parallel fashion, such as in bars 105 and 107; the resultant chromaticism lends a hip, modern sound. The octaves reappear in these two choruses, too. In bars 109–112, a pair of Cs are syncopated against the open sixth string, and the solo ends with a series of octaves, coming to rest on a handful of Gs.

Fig. 13

20 Full Band
21 Slow Demo meas. 49-128

Head

Moderately, in 2 ♩ = 120

*N.C.

*Chord symbols reflect overall harmony.

Copyright © 1963 Prestige Music
Copyright Renewed
International Copyright Secured   All Rights Reserved

Em7 B♭7 A7
Dm7 A♭7 G7 C C/E F F♯° C/G G7 C
Solo 1st Chorus 0:16
C Dm7 G7 C
P.M.
Dm7 G7 C
P.M.
Em7 A7 Dm7 G7 C C/E
Solo 2nd Chorus 0:33
F F♯° G N.C. C
P.M.
let ring

35
Dm7 G7 C Dm7 G7
let ring
let ring simile
40
C Em7 A7 Dm7 G7
45
C C/E F F♯° G
Solo 3rd Chorus 0:50
49
C Dm7 G7 C
53
Dm7 G7 C7
57
Em7 A7 Dm7 G7 C C/E

Solo 4th Chorus 1:08
F F♯° G C/G C
G C G
C Em7 A7 Dm7 G7
Solo 5th Chorus 1:25
C C/E F F♯° G F/G C
Dm7 G7 Dm7 G7 C Em7 A7

87
Dm7
G7
C
Em7
A7
91
Dm7
G7
C
C/E
F
F♯°
Solo 6th Chorus
1:43
95
G
C/G
G
C
99
G
C
103
G
Em7
A7

107
Dm7
G7
C
C/E
F
F♯○
111
G
Solo 7th Chorus
2:00
C
115
C♯○
C
119
B♭
Em7
B7
B♭7
A7♯9♯5
Dm7
A♭7
124
G7♯9
C
C/E
F
F♯○
C/G
Am7
Dm7
G7
mp
*w/ vol. knob

TANGERINE
from the Paramount Picture THE FLEET'S IN
(*Jazz Guitar: Jim Hall Trio*, 1957)
Words by Johnny Mercer
Music by Victor Schertzinger

Figure 14—Head and Solo

On his 1957 debut, *Jazz Guitar: Jim Hall Trio*, the guitarist demonstrated himself to already be a formidable soloist, as well as a sensitive ensemble player, leading a trio of pianist Carl Perkins and bassist Red Mitchell. (Oddly, a later pressing featured the overdubbed drums of Larry Bunker.) The set consists of Swing Era standards that, while the context is a bit conservative, nonetheless reveal that Hall had a mature voice even as his career was just getting started.

From *Jazz Guitar*, the tune "Tangerine" has a 32-bar form. It's built mainly around ii–V changes in the key of F major, with a modulation to A major in bars 13–16. (Incidentally, the chord progression is very similar to that of Cole Porter's "I Love You.") In the head, Hall is fairly faithful to the original melody. To add his own stamp, though, he approaches certain notes from a half step below (bars 2, 6, and 8) and throws in the occasional eighth-note triplet (bars 5 and 6). Also, for an infectious swing feel, Hall plays with extensive syncopation; for instance, although they were originally conceived squarely on the downbeats, bar 25's notes fall entirely on the offbeats.

In the first four bars of his solo, beginning in bar 33, rather than outlining the changes, Hall looks at the overall harmony and works his way down the F major scale (F–G–A–B♭–C–D–E) via a couple of syncopated phrases. Similarly, beginning in bar 37, he works within the scale, adding the ♭3 (A♭) for some cool blueness.

In bar 45, to hit the modulation to A major, Hall thinks more harmonically, hitting choice notes from each chord, starting with the 6th (F♯) of Amaj7, then, between bars 47 and 48, smoothly moving by half step from the Amaj7's 9th (B) to the Gm7's ♭3rd (B♭).

Bars 49–56 contain some nice motivic development. The phrase in bars 51–52 is a variation on the one in 49–50, played a diatonic 2nd lower. In bars 53–54, Hall plays a line that faintly echoes the standard "Tea for Two," and then cleverly transposes it up a major 2nd in the following two bars.

Starting in bar 59, Hall explores the note D with an interesting technique: he plays it on both string 3, at fret 7, and string 2, at fret 3; this makes for the sort of timbral effect that a saxophonist gets when he plays the same note with different fingerings. Note also the thoughtful use of space here. Hall displaces the D by an octave in bar 63, albeit without two fingerings, and, beginning in bar 62, ends his first chorus with another bluesy phrase.

Hall continues his second chorus in much the same manner. Some highlights: beginning in bar 73, a hip, double-picked line opens with the ♭3rd (B♭) and 7th (F♯) of the Gm7 chord, before smoothly arriving at the Fmaj7 chord's 7th (E) via the C7's ♯9th (D♯). As he did with the previous D note, Hall focuses on a lone A note in bars 77–78, then C in bars 83–84, shifting each note to various rhythmic positions. At the top of bar 85, Hall states an ascending, three-note chromatic motif that is developed nicely over the next several bars. In bar 93, Hall once again draws from the F major scale, playing an angular phrase. He brings the solo to a close in bar 96 with a line that reintroduces the bluesy ♭3.

Fig. 14

Head

Moderately fast Swing ♩ = 120

25
B♭maj7
Gm7
Em7♭5
A7♭9
Dm7
E7
29
Gm7
C7sus4
C7
Fmaj7
Solo 1st Chorus
0:32
33
Gm7
C7
Fmaj7
B♭maj7
Am7
D7
37
Gm7
C7
Gm7
C7
Am7
D7♭9
41
Gm7
C7
Fmaj7
B♭maj7
Bm7
E7
45
Amaj7
F♯m7
Bm7
E7
Amaj7
Gm7
C7

49 Gm7 C7 Fmaj7 B♭maj7 Am7 D7
53 Gm7 C7 Gm7 C7 Am7♭5 D7♭9
57 B♭maj7 Gm7 Em7♭5 A7♭9 Dm7 E7
61 Gm7 C7 Fmaj7 D7♭9
Solo 2nd Chorus 1:04
65 Gm7 C7 Fmaj7 B♭maj7 Am7 D7
69 Gm7 C7 Gm7 C7 Am7 D7♭9

73
Gm7
C7
Fmaj7
B♭maj7
Bm7
E7
77
Amaj7
F♯m7
Bm7
E7
Amaj7
Gm7
C7
81
Gm7
C7
Fmaj7
B♭maj7
Am7
D7
85
Gm7
C7
Gm7
C7
Am7♭5
D7♭9
89
B♭maj7
Gm7
Em7♭5
A7♭9
Dm7
E7
93
Gm7
C7
Fmaj7
D7♭9
(Piano Solo)

THINGS AIN'T WHAT THEY USED TO BE
(*Jazz Guitar: Jim Hall Trio,* 1957)
By Mercer Ellington

Figure 15—Head and Solo

While Jim Hall's style is strikingly modern, it is deeply rooted in the traditional sound of the blues. This is especially apparent in Hall's interpretation of the Mercer Ellington classic "Things Ain't What They Used to Be," from his 1957 debut album, *Jazz Guitar: Jim Hall Trio*, on which "Tangerine" (see page 56) also appears.

"Things Ain't What They Used to Be" is based on a 12-bar blues in D♭ major, played here with a neat, overlapping pair of ii–Vs in bars 8–11 (F7–B♭7–E♭m7–A♭7–D♭7). Hall kicks things off by playing the head twice, the first time accompanied by bassist Red Mitchell. The guitarist basically plays the melody as it was originally written but adds some bluesy, grace-note flourishes: in the D♭7 bars, a whole-step slide, from E♭ to the melody note F; and on the double stops, a half-step approach tone to each lower note.

As Hall restates the head, beginning in bar 13, pianist Carl Perkins joins in on the proceedings; notice the chromatically ascending 7♯9 chords that Perkins substitutes in bars 21 and 22. Hall starts his reiteration of the head the same way he originally played it, but at the end of bar 20, he raises the intensity by playing the melody up an octave. Then, beginning in bar 23, he sets up his three-chorus solo with a triplet-based line that comes mainly from the D♭ minor pentatonic scale (D♭–F♭–G♭–A♭–C♭).

In the first chorus, Hall improvises variations on the original melody. In bars 29 and 30, he plays major 3rd–based double stops from the D♭ blues scale (D♭–F♭–G♭–A♭♭–A♭–C♭), then, in bar 31, toys with both the ♭3rd (F♭/E) and 3rd (F) of the D♭7 chord using single notes. In bar 35, over the D♭7–B♭7 change, Hall plays a series of dyads that actually imply the progression D♭7–G♭–G♭m, with the 3rd (B♭ and B♭♭ in the bass on the latter two). Note the contrary motion between the lower and higher voices of the first two chords.

Beginning at the end of his first chorus and extending through the first several bars of his second, Hall has a conversation with himself, playing phrases that start and stop on the first string's fourth-fret A♭, and are answered by phrases that start and stop a perfect 5th lower, on the third string's sixth-fret D♭. In bars 40–43, Hall plays the note E♭ at two different positions—string 2, fret 4 and string 3, fret 8—requiring a large fret-hand stretch, but the nice contrast in timbre is worth the effort. Hall begins to conclude his second chorus in bar 44 with a predominantly pentatonic phrase.

In his third and final chorus, Hall makes the most out of a few simple phrases, the first of which is stated in the first half of bar 49. Similar to one found in his first chorus, this bluesy, ascending phrase contains both the ♭3 and 3, and is carried throughout the first several bars. Bar 52 contains an interesting move: Hall slides, via a half step, into a dyad (C♭–E♭) that implies a D♭9 chord (D♭–F–A♭–C♭–E♭), then plays a descending chromatic line (A♭–A♭♭–G♭–F) that sets up a D♭9 chord partial (F–C♭–E♭). First appearing on beat 2 of bar 53, an eighth-note triplet line (F♭–D♭–E♭) is played (except for a break in bar 54) until the beginning of bar 56, and answered in bar 57 by a time-honored, jazz-blues phrase.

Hall thinks more harmonically as he ends his solo, arpeggiating D♭ (D♭–F–A♭) and G♭ (G♭–B♭–D♭) triads in bar 59, approaching each 3rd with a half-step grace note. Then, on beats 1 and 2 of the final bar, Hall plays double stops, A♭–D♭ and G–D♭, that imply B♭m7 (B♭–D♭–F–A♭) and E♭7 (E♭–G–B♭–D♭) chords, respectively, delaying the final ii–V (E♭m7–A♭7) change by two beats.

Fig. 15

Head

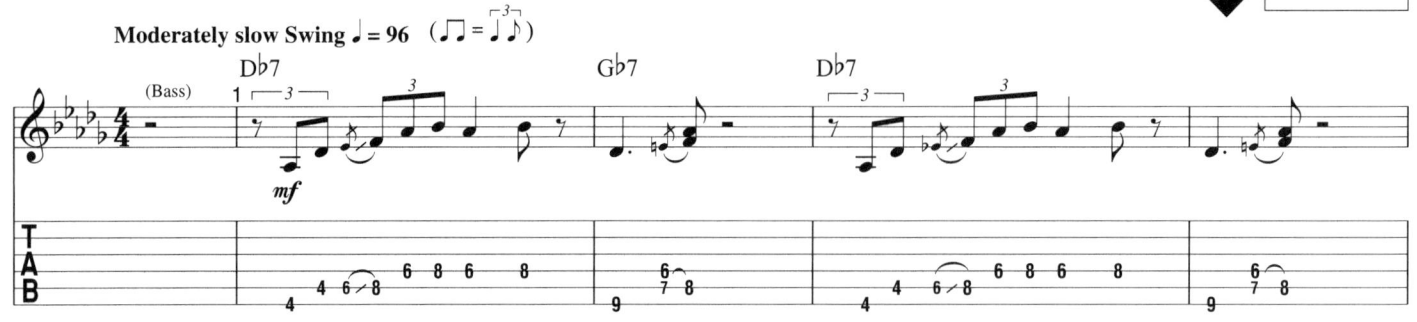

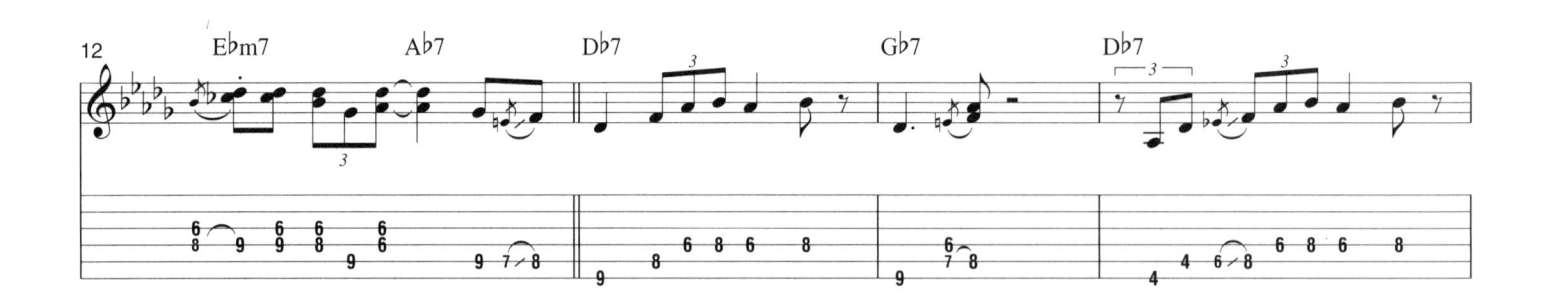

Moderately slow Swing ♩ = 96

F7 B♭7 E♭7♯9 E7♯9 F7♯9 G♭7♯9 G7♯9 A♭7♯9 D7 D♭7 B♭7
Solo 1st Chorus 1:00
E♭m7 A♭7 D♭7 G♭7 D♭7
G♭7
D♭7 F7 B♭7 E♭m7 A♭7
Solo 2nd Chorus 1:30
D♭7 B♭7 E♭m7 A♭7 D♭7 G♭7
D♭7 G♭7

43
D♭7
F7
B♭7
E♭m7
46
A♭7
D♭7
B♭7
E♭m7
A♭7
Solo 3rd Chorus 2:00
49
D♭7
G♭7
D♭7
52
G♭7
55
D♭7
F7
B♭7
Em7
58
A♭7
D♭7
G♭7
E♭m7
A♭7

WITHOUT A SONG
(*The Bridge*, 1962)

Words by William Rose and Edward Eliscu
Music by Vincent Youmans

Figure 16—Head

In 1962, tenor saxophonist Sonny Rollins—having come out of a three-year period of retirement—emerged with *The Bridge*, which was recorded with an awesome quartet that included guitarist Jim Hall, bassist Bob Cranshaw, and drummer Ben Riley. Particularly noteworthy with regard to this ensemble was the telekinetic interplay between Hall and Rollins; it was as if the two players were joined at the hip.

From that great album, "Without a Song" is based on a modified AABA form, in which each A-section is sixteen bars long, while the B-section is the standard eight. In bar 10 of the A-section, Rollins & Co. employ a neat harmonic trick: in place of the I chord, E♭maj7, they play a ii–V change (F♯m7–B7) that's located a half step above the ii–V (Fm7–B♭7) in bars 11–12.

Rollins takes the melody in the A-sections, while Hall adds simple, bluesy fills, colored with chromatic approach tones, such as the C♯ in bar 1 and the B♮ in bar 3. Hall also plays sparse, smartly voiced chord stabs. For example, there's a dyad in bar 12 that contains just the ♭7th (A♭) and root (B♭) of the B♭7 chord; similarly, bar 50's double stop is constructed from the 9th (G♯) and ♭3rd (A) of the F♯m7 chord—both notes are moved down by a half step on the "and" of beat 4, anticipating the following bar's Fm7 chord. Getting back to the first A-section, in bars 13–16, Hall plays three-note chords in a nice turnaround that travels diatonically downward: A♭maj7–Gm7–Fm7–E♭maj7–A♭m6–E♭. Variations of this progression appear throughout the tune.

Hall takes the lead in the B-section, from bars 33 to 40. He sticks fairly close to the original melody, articulating it with smooth slurs and throwing in a bit of syncopation for good measure before closing out the section with a slick descending slide, from F to D. Rollins then takes over for the final A-section (bars 41–56).

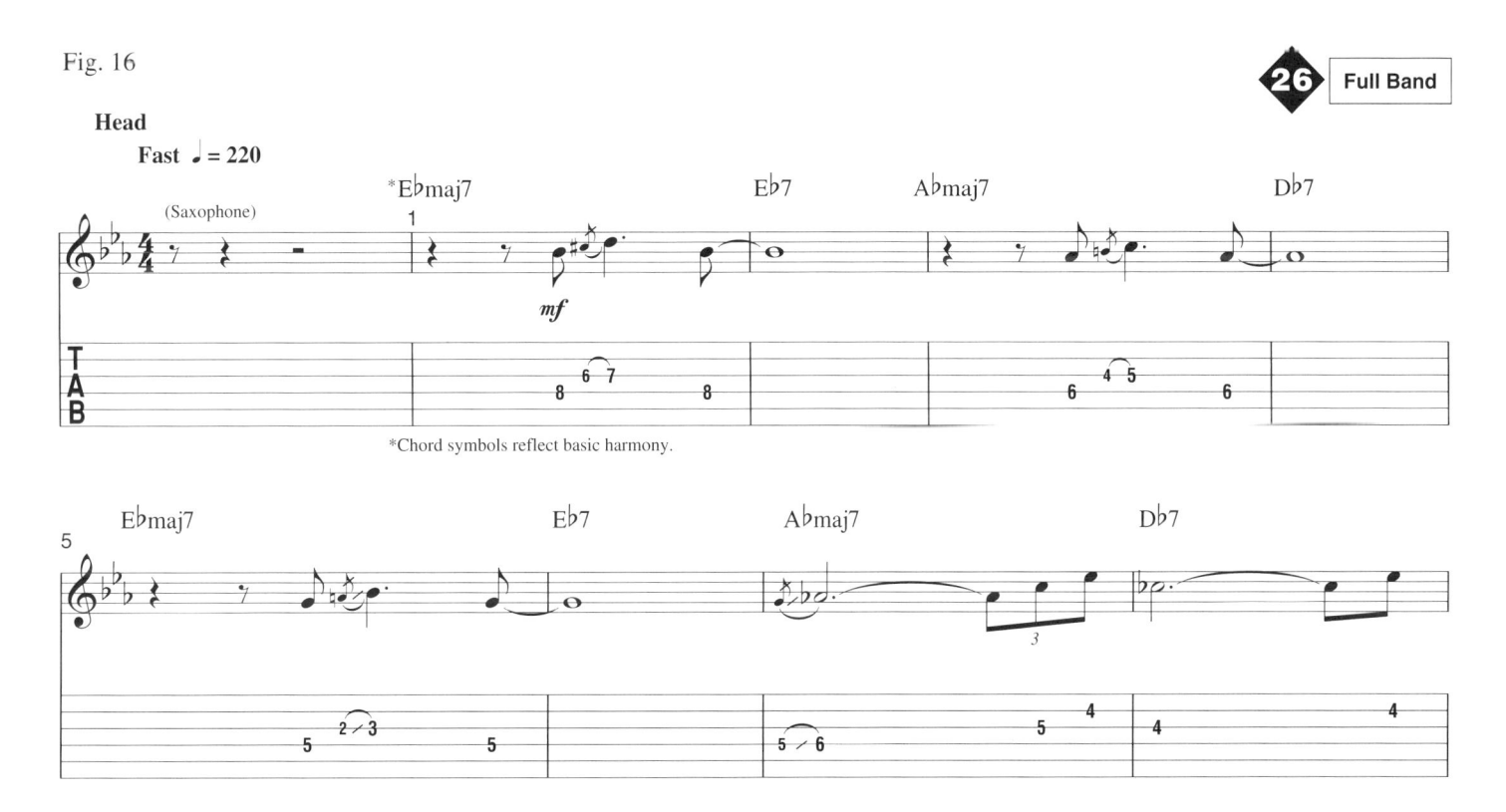

Ebmaj7 F#m7 B7 Fm7 Bb7
Ebmaj7 Abmaj7 Gm7 Fm7 Ebmaj7 Abm6 Eb Bb7
let ring
Ebmaj7 Eb7 Abmaj7 Db7
Ebmaj7 Eb7 Abmaj7 Db7
Ebmaj7 F#m7 B7 Fm7 Bb7
Ebmaj7 Abmaj7 Gm7 F7 Ebmaj7 Dbmaj7 Cm7
let ring

33 A♭maj7 Gm7 Fm7 B♭7 E♭maj7
37 Gm7 A7 D7 Gm7 C7 Fm7 B♭7
41 E♭maj7 E♭7 A♭maj7 D♭7
45 E♭maj7 E♭7 A♭maj7 D♭7
49 E♭maj7 F♯m7 B7 Fm7 B♭7
53 E♭maj7 Gm7 Fm7 E♭maj7 A♭m6 E♭
let ring
sim.

Figure 17—Solo (Chorus 1)

Hall begins his solo in the last bar of Cranshaw's bass solo. In bars 1 and 2, the guitarist outlines an E♭ triad using a rhythm that recalls Billy Strayhorn's "Take the A Train." In the next several bars, rather than outline the chords, he plays phrases drawn mainly from the E♭ major scale (E♭–F–G–A♭–B♭–C–D), flirting with the chromatic note F♯. But Hall is still conscious of the chords; for example, he nails the E♭7's ♭7th (D♭) on the downbeat of bar 6.

In bar 7, Hall begins to think more harmonically, employing a descending A♭add9 (B♭–A♭–E♭–C) arpeggio on beats 3 and 4, which connects, via a half step, to the ♭7 (C♭) of bar 8's D♭7 chord. Similarly, the E♭ arpeggio (B♭–G–E♭–B♭) on beats 3 and 4 of bar 9 smoothly leads into F♯m7's ♭3rd (A), which then leaps dramatically up a major 10th, to the chord's 5th (C♯).

Beginning in bar 13, Hall plays a constant E♭ note (string 3, fret 8) above the chromatically ascending G–A♭–A line; at the same time, Cranshaw plays the chromatically descending line E♭–D♭–C–B. Together, these parts imply a cool blues turnaround: E♭7–E♭/D♭–A♭/C–B7.

The blueness continues in the second A-section, where Hall plays a minor 3rd (G-to-B♭) motif in the first several bars, sliding into the G by a half step each time. In bar 21, the motif is transposed up a 4th, to C–E♭, and decorated with double grace notes (B♭ and B♮). Hall works with some more 3rds in bars 26–27, this time a chromatically descending series of major 3rds (D–B♭, C♯–A, and C–A♭), and, in bar 29, he closes out the A-section with another blues turnaround.

Hall begins the bridge of his first chorus (bar 33) by simply outlining an A♭ major triad (A♭–C–E♭). In bars 34 and 35, he takes another half-step approach, moving from the Gm7 chord's 9th (A) to the Fm7 chord's ♭3rd (A♭). This is followed by an angular reverse rake, the notes of which (G, D, and A♭) belong to a B♭13 chord (B♭–D–F–A♭–C–E♭–G). In bar 38 Hall plays some chord stabs that contain just the essential information: the ♭7th (G) and 3rd (C♯) of A7 and the 3rd (F♯), ♭7th (C), and ♭9th (E♭) of D7.

The final A-section of Hall's first chorus contains all the materials introduced so far: bluesy approach tones (bar 41), downward arpeggios (bar 45), and two-note chords (bar 46). He closes out the chorus with a series of four-note block chords, introducing a new, jazzier turnaround in bars 55–56 (E♭9–G♭9–F9–E9).

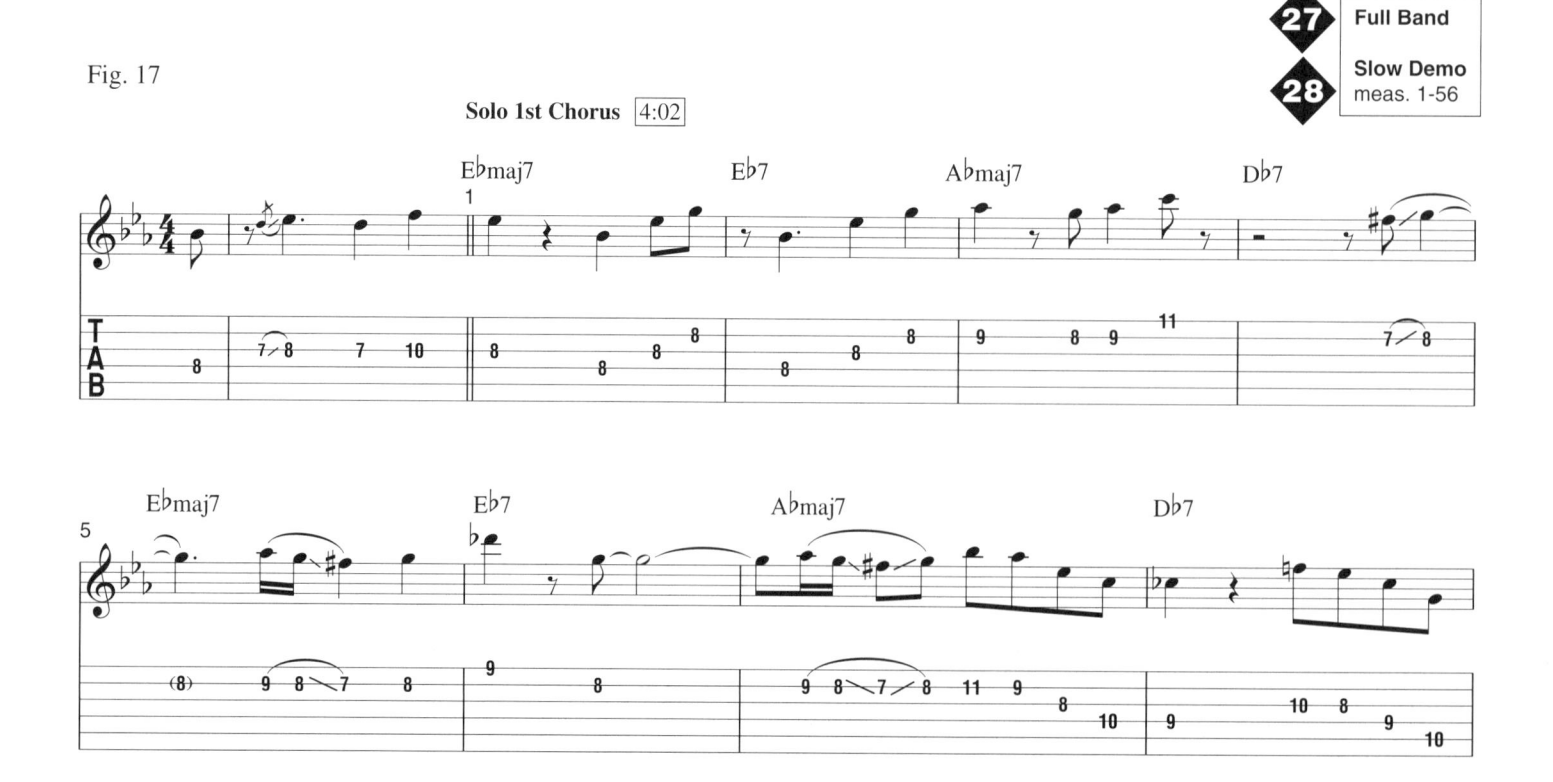

Fig. 17

Solo 1st Chorus [4:02]

27 Full Band
28 Slow Demo meas. 1-56

E♭maj7 F♯m7 B7 Fm7 B♭7
E♭7 E♭/D♭ A♭/C B7 B♭7 E♭7
steady gliss.
E♭maj7 E♭7 A♭maj7 D♭7
E♭maj7 E♭7 A♭maj7 D♭7
E♭maj7 F♯m7 B7 Fm7 B♭7
E♭7 E♭/D♭ A♭/C B7 B♭7 E♭7

33
A♭maj7
Gm7
Fm7
B♭7
E♭maj7
37
Gm7
A7
D7
Gm7
C7
Fm7
B♭7
41
E♭maj7
E♭7
A♭maj7
D♭7
45
E♭maj7
E♭7
A♭maj7
D♭7
49
E♭maj7
F♯m7
B7
Fm7
B♭7
53
E♭7
A♭
A°7
E♭9
G♭9
F9
E9

YOU'D BE SO NICE TO COME HOME TO
from SOMETHING TO SHOUT ABOUT
(*Concierto*, 1975)
Words and Music by Cole Porter

Figure 18—Head and Solo 1

    Recorded in 1975, Jim Hall's *Concierto* is considered the finest album ever recorded on the CTI label. On the recording, Hall is joined by a stellar team of musicians: trumpeter Chet Baker, alto saxophonist Paul Desmond, pianist Roland Hanna, bassist Ron Carter, and drummer Steve Gadd. While the album's centerpiece is an arrangement of Spanish composer Joaquìn Rodrigo's *Concierto de Aranjuez*, Hall's lines on the Cole Porter standard "You'd Be So Nice to Come Home To" offer a most excellent glimpse at the guitarist's improvisational style.

    Played in G minor, the tune has a 32-bar form, containing two 16-bar sections with identical changes in the first 8 bars of each. The recording's driving tempo of 224 beats per minute showcases Hall's dexterity on the guitar. He plays the head in single notes, embellishing the original melody with various jazzy touches, including legato slides and chromatic approach tones, such as the G♯ grace note in bar 3 and the C♯ lower-neighbor tone in bar 9. Note the bluesy, half-step bend in bar 14. An uncommon move for a jazz guitarist, this technique will appear several more times in the solos. Starting in bar 30, Hall ends the head by improvising a characteristically modern phrase based on octaves and 4ths, and an eighth note/dotted–quarter note rhythmic motif.

    In the first chorus of his solo, Hall plays coherent lines by developing various rhythmic motifs through the changes. The first one—like the one at the end of the head but occurring over the barline and notated as an eighth note followed by an eighth note tied to a quarter—begins in bar 36 and ends in 40, then reappears in bar 54. Notice how smoothly Hall negotiates the chords, using minimal movement between the first and second eighth notes of each motif. For example, on the "and" of beat 4 of bar 36, he plays an E grace note, raising it a half step, to F, to fit the Fm7 chord on the "and" of beat 2 of bar 37. Treated with similar melodic finesse, another rhythmic motif can be found in bars 57–60. Here, Hall—known for his judicious use of space—separates pairs of eighth notes with two beats of rests.

    Beginning in the last bar of the first chorus, and extending into measures 1–4 of the second chorus, Hall downwardly arpeggiates a B♭maj7 chord (B♭–D–F–A) with a slippery rhythmic feel, incorporating eighth-note triplets and 16ths. This works well, as Hanna comps sparsely and the blanket harmony is Gm7. (A B♭maj7 chord is essentially the top four notes of a Gm9 chord [G–B♭–D–F–A].) Hall moves the entire shape down a whole step for the Fm7 chord in bar 69.

    Hall's trademark less-is-more approach is further evidenced in the extensive rests of bars 73, 76, and 77. The half-step bend reappears in bar 78, followed by a complementary blues phrase derived from the G minor pentatonic scale (G–B♭–C–D–F). And in bar 89, the pair-of-eighths rhythmic motif resurfaces, this time separated by rests of one beat, as opposed to two. Then there's that half-step bend again, in bar 93.

    Hall begins the last phrase of his solo with an odd note choice—the major 7th (A♭/G♯) of bar 96's Am7♭5 chord. While the note is technically incorrect, it adds an exotic flavor; this sort of fleeting dissonance can be found in the work of any great jazz improviser. Getting back on track, the A♭ is followed by notes belonging to the G blues scale (G–B♭–C–D♭–D–F), and Hall ends his solo with a single C note, in the first bar of Desmond's saxophone solo.

Fig. 18

Head

Moderately fast Swing ♩ = 112 (♫ = ♩♪)

29 Full Band

30 Slow Demo meas. 33-97

Em7♭5 A7 B♭maj7 Am7♭5 D7 Gm7
B♭maj7/F Gm7 G♭7 F7 B♭maj7
Solo 1–1st Chorus
0:37
Gm7 Am7♭5 D7 Gm7
Fm7 B♭7 E♭maj7
Am7♭5 D7 E♭7 D7 Gm7
Em7♭5 B♭m7 E♭7 Am7♭5 D7

49
Gm7
Am7♭5
D7
Gm7
53
Fm7
B♭7
E♭maj7
57
Em7♭5
A7
B♭maj7
Am7♭5
D7
Gm7
61
B♭maj7/F
Gm7
G♭7
F7
B♭maj7
Am7♭5
D7
Solo 1–2nd Chorus
1:12
65
Gm7
Am7♭5
D7
Gm7
69
Fm7
B♭7
E♭maj7

73
Am7♭5
D7
E♭7
D7
Gm7
77
Em7♭5
B♭m7
E♭7
Am7♭5
D7
1/2
81
Gm7
Am7♭5
D7
Gm7
85
Fm7
B♭7
E♭maj7
89
Em7♭5
A7
B♭maj7
Am7♭5
D7
Gm7
93
B♭maj7/F
Gm7
G♭7
F7
B♭maj7
Am7♭5
D7
1/2

Figure 19—Solo 2

    Picking up on a rhythm played by Carter at the end of his bass solo, Hall carries the motif—two eighth notes placed on offbeats, followed by a quarter note on a downbeat—throughout the first section of his second solo. The first four bars are drawn from the G melodic minor scale (G–A–B♭–C–D–E–F♯), while bars 5–16 are based more on arpeggios. Beginning on beat 3 of bar 6, for example, Hall plays notes belonging to an E♭maj7 chord (E♭–G–B♭–D), and in bar 10 he plays an E♭°7 arpeggio (enharmonically written as E♭–F♯–A–C), which, in context, functions as D7♭9 (D–F♯–A–C–E♭).

    In the second 16 bars, Hall again plays with space, laying down phrases separated by two beats of rest or more and, similar to his first solo, sometimes incorporating pairs of eighth notes (see bars 19 and 20). In bar 29 is yet another half-step bend, and beginning in bar 31, the solo, like the first one, ends with a phrase from the G blues scale. Here, the chromatically descending notes D, D♭, and C neatly connect the B♭maj7, Am7♭5, and D7 chords, respectively.

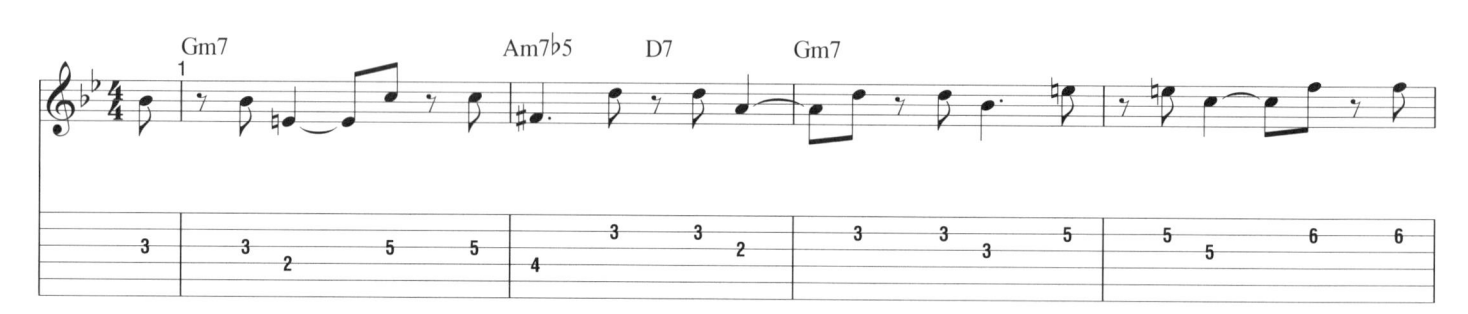

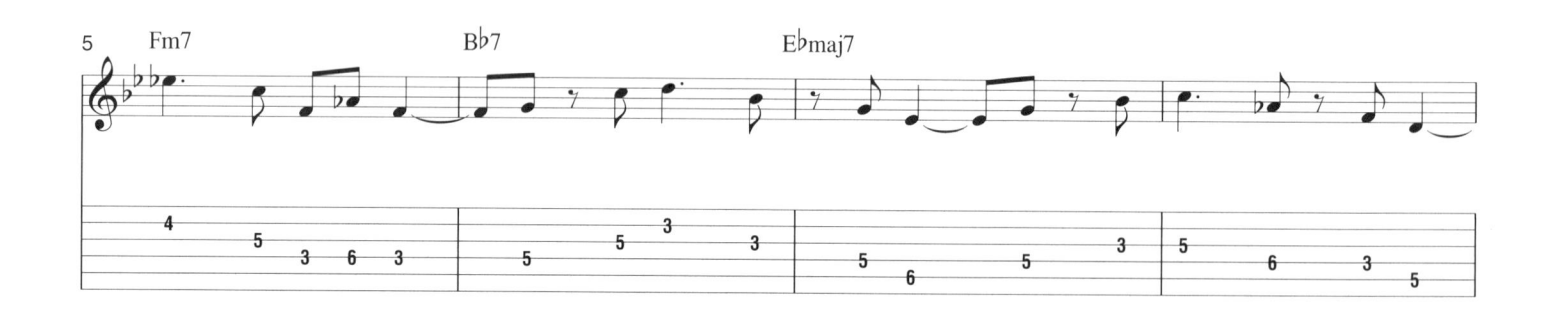

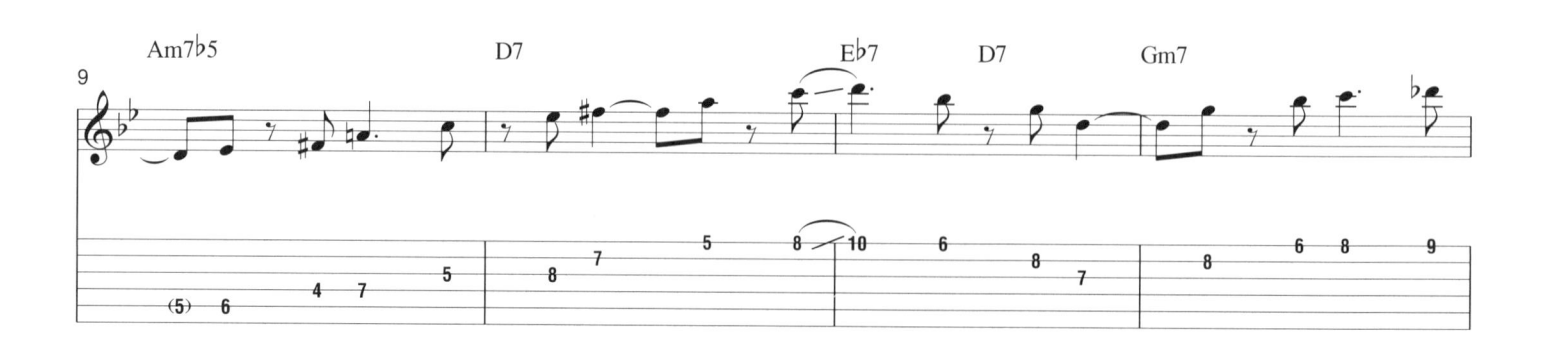

13
Em7♭5
B♭m7
E♭7
Am7♭5
D7
17
Gm7
Am7♭5
D7
Gm7
21
Fm7
B♭7
E♭maj7
25
Em7♭5
A7
B♭maj7
Am7♭5
D7
Gm7
29
B♭maj7/F
Gm7
G♭7
F7
B♭maj7
Am7♭5
D7
1/2

Guitar Notation Legend

Guitar music can be notated three different ways: on a *musical staff*, in *tablature*, and in *rhythm slashes*.

RHYTHM SLASHES are written above the staff. Strum chords in the rhythm indicated. Use the chord diagrams found at the top of the first page of the transcription for the appropriate chord voicings. Round noteheads indicate single notes.

THE MUSICAL STAFF shows pitches and rhythms and is divided by bar lines into measures. Pitches are named after the first seven letters of the alphabet.

TABLATURE graphically represents the guitar fingerboard. Each horizontal line represents a a string, and each number represents a fret.

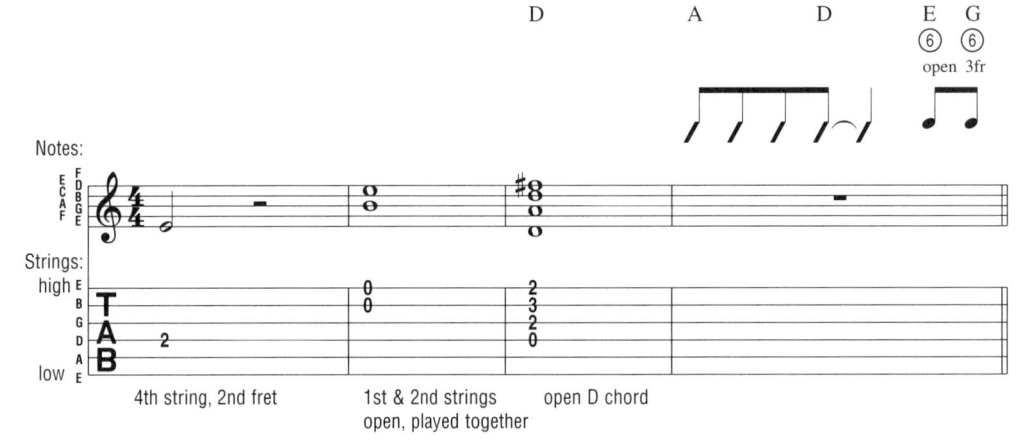

Definitions for Special Guitar Notation

HALF-STEP BEND: Strike the note and bend up 1/2 step.

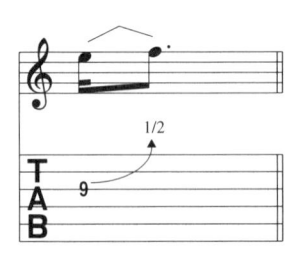

WHOLE-STEP BEND: Strike the note and bend up one step.

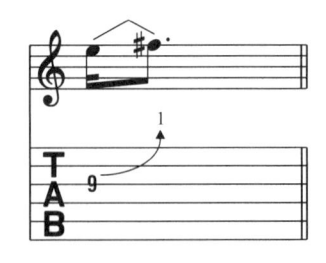

GRACE NOTE BEND: Strike the note and immediately bend up as indicated.

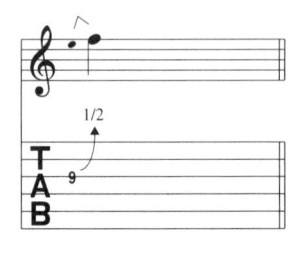

SLIGHT (MICROTONE) BEND: Strike the note and bend up 1/4 step.

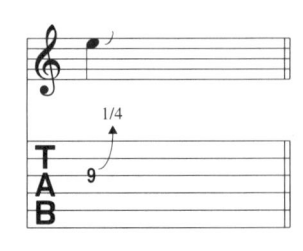

BEND AND RELEASE: Strike the note and bend up as indicated, then release back to the original note. Only the first note is struck.

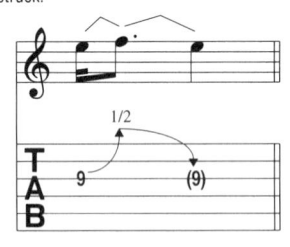

PRE-BEND: Bend the note as indicated, then strike it.

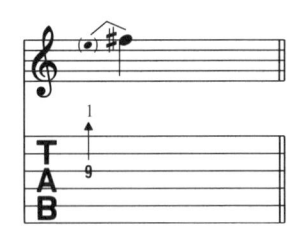

PRE-BEND AND RELEASE: Bend the note as indicated. Strike it and release the bend back to the original note.

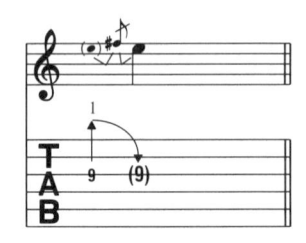

UNISON BEND: Strike the two notes simultaneously and bend the lower note up to the pitch of the higher.

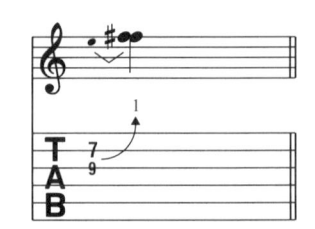

VIBRATO: The string is vibrated by rapidly bending and releasing the note with the fretting hand.

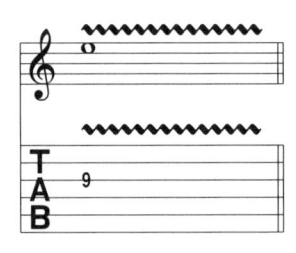

WIDE VIBRATO: The pitch is varied to a greater degree by vibrating with the fretting hand.

HAMMER-ON: Strike the first (lower) note with one finger, then sound the higher note (on the same string) with another finger by fretting it without picking.

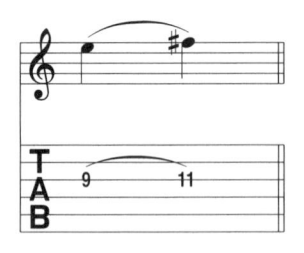

PULL-OFF: Place both fingers on the notes to be sounded. Strike the first note and without picking, pull the finger off to sound the second (lower) note.

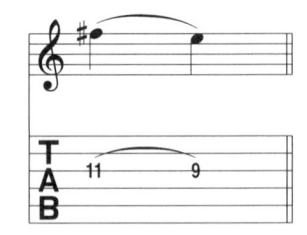

LEGATO SLIDE: Strike the first note and then slide the same fret-hand finger up or down to the second note. The second note is not struck.

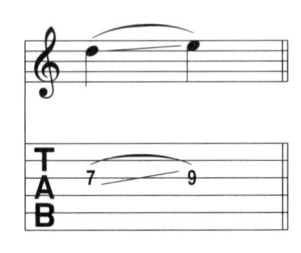

SHIFT SLIDE: Same as legato slide, except the second note is struck.

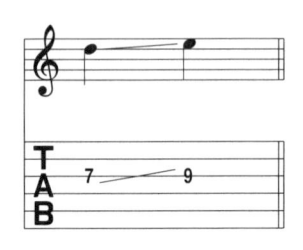

TRILL: Very rapidly alternate between the notes indicated by continuously hammering on and pulling off.

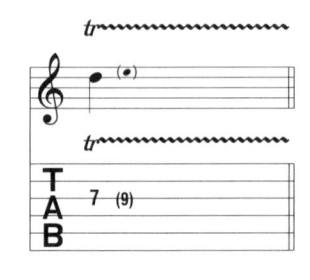

TAPPING: Hammer ("tap") the fret indicated with the pick-hand index or middle finger and pull off to the note fretted by the fret hand.

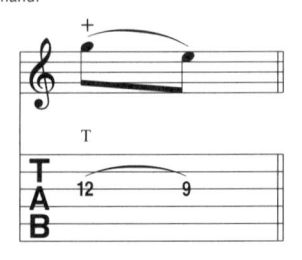

NATURAL HARMONIC: Strike the note while the fret-hand lightly touches the string directly over the fret indicated.

PINCH HARMONIC: The note is fretted normally and a harmonic is produced by adding the edge of the thumb or the tip of the index finger of the pick hand to the normal pick attack.

HARP HARMONIC: The note is fretted normally and a harmonic is produced by gently resting the pick hand's index finger directly above the indicated fret (in parentheses) while the pick hand's thumb or pick assists by plucking the appropriate string.

PICK SCRAPE: The edge of the pick is rubbed down (or up) the string, producing a scratchy sound.

MUFFLED STRINGS: A percussive sound is produced by laying the fret hand across the string(s) without depressing, and striking them with the pick hand.

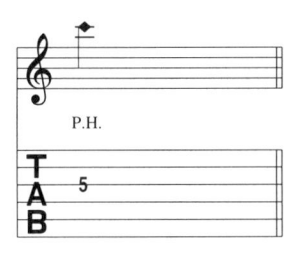

PALM MUTING: The note is partially muted by the pick hand lightly touching the string(s) just before the bridge.

RAKE: Drag the pick across the strings indicated with a single motion.

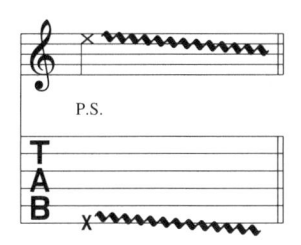

TREMOLO PICKING: The note is picked as rapidly and continuously as possible.

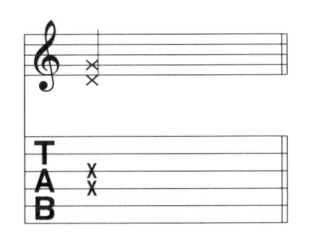

ARPEGGIATE: Play the notes of the chord indicated by quickly rolling them from bottom to top.

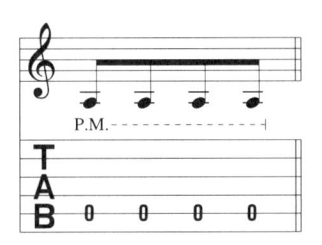

VIBRATO BAR DIVE AND RETURN: The pitch of the note or chord is dropped a specified number of steps (in rhythm) then returned to the original pitch.

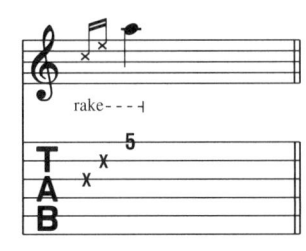

VIBRATO BAR SCOOP: Depress the bar just before striking the note, then quickly release the bar.

VIBRATO BAR DIP: Strike the note and then immediately drop a specified number of steps, then release back to the original pitch.

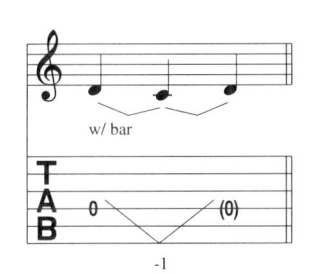

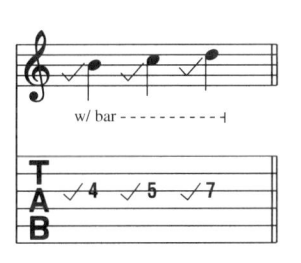

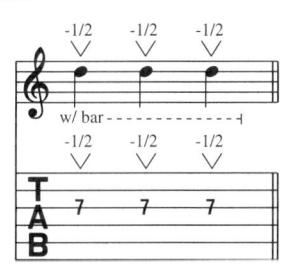

Additional Musical Definitions

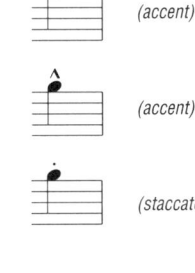

(accent)	Accentuate note (play it louder)	
(accent)	Accentuate note with great intensity	
(staccato)	Play the note short	
⊓	Downstroke	
V	Upstroke	
D.S. al Coda	Go back to the sign (𝄋), then play until the measure marked "**To Coda**," then skip to the section labelled "**Coda**."	
D.C. al Fine	Go back to the beginning of the song and play until the measure marked "**Fine**" (end).	

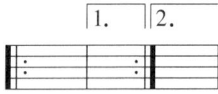

- **Rhy. Fig.** — Label used to recall a recurring accompaniment pattern (usually chordal).
- **Riff** — Label used to recall composed, melodic lines (usually single notes) which recur.
- **Fill** — Label used to identify a brief melodic figure which is to be inserted into the arrangement.
- **Rhy. Fill** — A chordal version of a Fill.
- **tacet** — Instrument is silent (drops out).
- Repeat measures between signs.
- When a repeated section has different endings, play the first ending only the first time and the second ending only the second time.

NOTE: Tablature numbers in parentheses mean:
1. The note is being sustained over a system (note in standard notation is tied), or
2. The note is sustained, but a new articulation (such as a hammer-on, pull-off, slide or vibrato) begins, or
3. The note is a barely audible "ghost" note (note in standard notation is also in parentheses).

GUITAR *signature licks*

Signature Licks book/CD packs provide a step-by-step breakdown of "right from the record" riffs, licks, and solos so you can jam along with your favorite bands. They contain performance notes and an overview of each artist's or group's style, with note-for-note transcriptions in notes and tab. The CDs feature full-band demos at both normal and slow speeds.

ACOUSTIC CLASSICS
00695864 .... $19.95

BEST OF ACOUSTIC GUITAR
00695640 .... $19.95

AEROSMITH 1973-1979
00695106 .... $22.95

AEROSMITH 1979-1998
00695219 .... $22.95

BEST OF AGGRO-METAL
00695592 .... $19.95

BEST OF CHET ATKINS
00695752 .... $22.95

THE BEACH BOYS DEFINITIVE COLLECTION
00695683 .... $22.95

BEST OF THE BEATLES FOR ACOUSTIC GUITAR
00695453 .... $22.95

THE BEATLES BASS
00695283 .... $22.95

THE BEATLES FAVORITES
00695096 .... $24.95

THE BEATLES HITS
00695049 .... $24.95

BEST OF GEORGE BENSON
00695418 .... $22.95

BEST OF BLACK SABBATH
00695249 .... $22.95

BEST OF BLINK-182
00695704 .... $22.95

BEST OF BLUES GUITAR
00695846 .... $19.95

BLUES GUITAR CLASSICS
00695177 .... $19.95

BLUES/ROCK GUITAR MASTERS
00695348 .... $19.95

KENNY BURRELL
00695830 .... $22.95

BEST OF CHARLIE CHRISTIAN
00695584 .... $22.95

BEST OF ERIC CLAPTON
00695038 .... $24.95

ERIC CLAPTON – THE BLUESMAN
00695040 .... $22.95

ERIC CLAPTON – FROM THE ALBUM UNPLUGGED
00695250 .... $24.95

BEST OF CREAM
00695251 .... $22.95

CREEDANCE CLEARWATER REVIVAL
00695924 .... $22.95

DEEP PURPLE – GREATEST HITS
00695625 .... $22.95

THE BEST OF DEF LEPPARD
00696516 .... $22.95

THE DOORS
00695373 .... $22.95

FAMOUS ROCK GUITAR SOLOS
00695590 .... $19.95

BEST OF FOO FIGHTERS
00695481 .... $22.95

ROBBEN FORD
00695903 .... $22.95

GREATEST GUITAR SOLOS OF ALL TIME
00695301 .... $19.95

BEST OF GRANT GREEN
00695747 .... $22.95

GUITAR INSTRUMENTAL HITS
00695309 .... $19.95

GUITAR RIFFS OF THE '60S
00695218 .... $19.95

BEST OF GUNS N' ROSES
00695183 .... $22.95

HARD ROCK SOLOS
00695591 .... $19.95

JIMI HENDRIX
00696560 .... $24.95

HOT COUNTRY GUITAR
00695580 .... $19.95

BEST OF JAZZ GUITAR
00695586 .... $24.95

ERIC JOHNSON
00699317 .... $24.95

ROBERT JOHNSON
00695264 .... $22.95

THE ESSENTIAL ALBERT KING
00695713 .... $22.95

B.B. KING – THE DEFINITIVE COLLECTION
00695635 .... $22.95

THE KINKS
00695553 .... $22.95

BEST OF KISS
00699413 .... $22.95

MARK KNOPFLER
00695178 .... $22.95

LYNYRD SKYNYRD
00695872 .... $24.95

BEST OF YNGWIE MALMSTEEN
00695669 .... $22.95

BEST OF PAT MARTINO
00695632 .... $22.95

WES MONTGOMERY
00695387 .... $24.95

BEST OF NIRVANA
00695483 .... $24.95

THE OFFSPRING
00695852 .... $24.95

VERY BEST OF OZZY OSBOURNE
00695431 .... $22.95

BEST OF JOE PASS
00695730 .... $22.95

PINK FLOYD – EARLY CLASSICS
00695566 .... $22.95

THE POLICE
00695724 .... $22.95

THE GUITARS OF ELVIS
00696507 .... $22.95

BEST OF QUEEN
00695097 .... $24.95

BEST OF RAGE AGAINST THE MACHINE
00695480 .... $24.95

RED HOT CHILI PEPPERS
00695173 .... $22.95

RED HOT CHILI PEPPERS – GREATEST HITS
00695828 .... $24.95

BEST OF DJANGO REINHARDT
00695660 .... $24.95

BEST OF ROCK
00695884 .... $19.95

BEST OF ROCK 'N' ROLL GUITAR
00695559 .... $19.95

BEST OF ROCKABILLY GUITAR
00695785 .... $19.95

THE ROLLING STONES
00695079 .... $24.95

BEST OF JOE SATRIANI
00695216 .... $22.95

BEST OF SILVERCHAIR
00695488 .... $22.95

THE BEST OF SOUL GUITAR
00695703 .... $19.95

BEST OF SOUTHERN ROCK
00695560 .... $19.95

ROD STEWART
00695663 .... $22.95

BEST OF SURF GUITAR
00695822 .... $19.95

BEST OF SYSTEM OF A DOWN
00695788 .... $22.95

STEVE VAI
00673247 .... $22.95

STEVE VAI – ALIEN LOVE SECRETS: THE NAKED VAMPS
00695223 .... $22.95

STEVE VAI – FIRE GARDEN: THE NAKED VAMPS
00695166 .... $22.95

STEVE VAI – THE ULTRA ZONE: NAKED VAMPS
00695684 .... $22.95

STEVIE RAY VAUGHAN
00699316 .... $24.95

THE GUITAR STYLE OF STEVIE RAY VAUGHAN
00695155 .... $24.95

BEST OF THE VENTURES
00695772 .... $19.95

THE WHO
00695561 .... $22.95

BEST OF ZZ TOP
00695738 .... $24.95

Complete descriptions and songlists online!

FOR MORE INFORMATION, SEE YOUR LOCAL MUSIC DEALER, OR WRITE TO:

HAL•LEONARD® CORPORATION
7777 W. BLUEMOUND RD. P.O. BOX 13819 MILWAUKEE, WI 53213

www.halleonard.com
Prices, contents and availability subject to change without notice.